SPIRITED
SCHOOLROOM

The Earthly lessons and adventures of a healer.

MARTY MONTES

BALBOA.
PRESS
A DIVISION OF HAY HOUSE

Balboa Press books may be ordered through booksellers or by contacting:

Balboa Press
A Division of Hay House
1663 Liberty Drive
Bloomington, IN 47403
www.balboapress.com
1 (877) 407-4847

Because of the dynamic nature of the Internet, any web addresses or links contained in this book may have changed since publication and may no longer be valid. The views expressed in this work are solely those of the author and do not necessarily reflect the views of the publisher, and the publisher hereby disclaims any responsibility for them.

The author of this book does not dispense medical advice or prescribe the use of any technique as a form of treatment for physical, emotional, or medical problems without the advice of a physician, either directly or indirectly. The intent of the author is only to offer information of a general nature to help you in your quest for emotional and spiritual well-being. In the event you use any of the information in this book for yourself, which is your constitutional right, the author and the publisher assume no responsibility for your actions.

Any people depicted in stock imagery provided by Thinkstock are models, and such images are being used for illustrative purposes only. Certain stock imagery © Thinkstock.

Print information available on the last page.

ISBN: 978-1-5043-3650-5 (sc)
ISBN: 978-1-5043-3652-9 (hc)
ISBN: 978-1-5043-3651-2 (e)

Library of Congress Control Number: 2015910819

Balboa Press rev. date: 07/07/2015

To Marcy, my mother.

Thank you for your dreams and visits.
I miss your sense of humor and your great laugh.
May you continue to make others laugh wherever you may be.

With love and peace, your son,
Marty

CONTENTS

Acknowledgments ix

Preface xi

Section 1.   The Divine Blueprint 1

    Chapter 1.   Revelation 3

    Chapter 2.   Freedom 17

    Chapter 3.   Visitors 27

    Chapter 4.   Fate 39

    Chapter 5.   Reunion 48

    Chapter 6.   Testimony 60

    Chapter 7.   Pluto 67

    Chapter 8.   Shock 86

    Chapter 9.   Surreal 94

    Chapter 10. Leap 112

    Chapter 11. Patience 125

    Chapter 12. India 138

    Chapter 13. Lessons 146

    Chapter 14. Acceptance 161

    Chapter 15. Surrender 169

Section 2. The Divine Gifts 173
    Chapter 16. Dreams 175
    Chapter 17. Healing 181
    Chapter 18. Choice 195
    Chapter 19. Signs 201
    Chapter 20. Silence 209
    Chapter 21. Thoughts 216
    Chapter 22. Purpose 226

Bibliography 235

Acknowledgments

I send big hugs to my family and true friends for showing me your love and accepting me as I am. My relationships with you are the basis for my happiness.

I give thanks to all those who helped me with editing and providing creative ideas, especially Maggie. This book project has taken more than a decade to manifest, so I'm very excited to finally see it in print and to share it with the world.

I extend my gratitude to the staff at Balboa Press for their support and insight and, more importantly, for publishing this book.

PREFACE

A master spirit told me, "You are a student of everything and a victim of nothing."

They say when the student's ready, the teacher appears. I'm here to testify that this philosophy is true. The master spirit's message came in the nick of time, when I was about to embark on an intense astrological transit that touched my soul. The deeply emotional and transformational experiences that unfolded during this celestial event erected a new spiritual foundation that gave me meaningful purpose and a fulfilling mission.

What is the *real* purpose for living on earth? Why is life itself so tough? Those and many more thought-provoking questions are answered in this book.

I've learned that souls who incarnated to teach and help others chose a demanding blueprint filled with many spiritual lessons, particularly forgiveness, which was not one of my favorites to learn but is one of the most powerful. My journey out of the dark and into the light was not easy. However, each experience did mold my character and expand my awareness. While I used to frown upon obstacles and challenges, I now view them as opportunities to grow and to embrace the teachings.

Spirited Schoolroom is filled with true stories and inspirational teachings. Only names, physical descriptions, and some locations have been changed to honor others' privacy. The book describes incredible visits from the spirit of my friend who died on September 11. It is my hope that some of these stories will leave you inspired and healed.

The book is filled with humor, prophetic dreams, messages, miracles, wisdom, and spiritual secrets. It will show that peace, hope, joy, honesty, laughter, happiness, optimism, creativity, gratitude, respect, loyalty, courage, faith, abundance, and love have no gender. This book also confirms without a doubt that we are all connected under one consciousness.

Spirited Schoolroom was born of divine inspiration. I'm blessed to be an instrument for the universe, and I hope that your spiritual journey provides gratification and the fulfillment of your purpose and mission.

The universe is designed to help you succeed, not break you down. Yes, you will be knocked down and feel battered and bruised, but you'll only *perceive* failure if you don't pick yourself up and try again. Knock-downs are merely lessons to help you succeed. This was also one of the toughest lessons I've had to learn.

I enjoyed sharing my personal story. It is my deepest desire to inspire you to pursue your dreams and live the greatest life you're willing to partake in. Create from the depths of your imagination, and experience all the love that the universe makes available to you.

With love,
Marty

THE DIVINE
BLUEPRINT

CHAPTER ONE

REVELATION

Three days after the death of my beloved cat, Cashmere, I had the following life-changing dream that awakened and shifted my consciousness:

I was having trouble falling asleep one evening. I tossed and turned for a few minutes and then decided to get up. When I entered the living room, I was shocked to see Cashmere grooming herself on the couch, illuminated in white light. She looked up at me with those piercing blue Siamese eyes and walked toward me.

I could not believe I was looking at my cat. She'd only died three days before. As she approached, I knelt in silence. I extended my left hand to her and looked in the opposite direction in denial. Then I turned back to her, and she walked through my hand. I felt her essence—her energy, her spirit—go through my hand, up my shoulders, and throughout my body. It was just incredible.

I walked back to the other side of the room. When I turned around, I could still see Cashmere, illuminated. Suddenly I heard a gentle female voice say, "We don't die. Energy transforms." In that moment, I realized Cashmere would always be around me.

I decided to get some fresh air, so I walked outside and sat on the front steps. The atmosphere outside felt very hostile, and I heard neighbors yelling at each other. I reflected for a short while about the sensation of Cashmere going through me and then went back inside. As I walked upstairs to my bedroom, I noticed my illuminated cat had followed me. She jumped onto my bed to sleep with me.

Then I was transported upward in a white elevator surrounded by many spirits, or energy fields, that did not conform to a specific shape or size. It seemed that the vibration around them determined the evolution of that energy. I felt peaceful and received impressions from these energy fields. I was told, "This planet, Earth, is only one of a wider circle of learning."

I strongly believed there were other places of being. At that point, the elevator stopped. The right side opened, and I saw planet Earth below me to the right. I found it odd that the elevator had opened from the side and not from the front. Then I was impressed with another telepathic declaration: "The reason for such a great number of souls on the planet is that earth is the greatest schoolroom for learning the most lessons of the soul. Many choose to incarnate on earth because they can learn the most there in the shortest period of time."

After that statement the elevator closed again, and I felt myself quickly ascending. When the elevator stopped, this time the front doors opened. A brilliant blue light blinded me, and it seemed to be vibrating around a male energy or presence. I strongly felt that it was a spirit guide, an evolved soul. I sensed that only another evolved energy could tune in to such a high vibration. As I stood mesmerized by the presence, the evolved spirit looked at me and entered the elevator, and the door closed.

I woke up from this dream at 2:10 a.m. As I opened my eyes, I smelled burning wax and knew that my candle had just burned out. *What a coincidence that I woke just as my candle finished burning,* I thought. I lay in bed thinking about my dream. *Earth is just a schoolroom.*

Well, that would explain why I had to experience some of the worst and most painful earthly conditions. I felt comforted that Cashmere had made it to the other side and would always be with me. I then sat up in bed, turned on the lamp, and recorded this incredible dream in my dream journal.

After writing it down, I reread it a couple of times, in awe of what had taken place. *Did I just leave my body and go on an incredible journey?* Yes, and yes! I looked over my description and analyzed the dream. The quiet inside my home versus the hostility outside indicated that peace could only come from within. Looking externally for peace would only bring more discomfort. Cashmere was illuminated in white light, a sign that she was in pure spiritual form—happy and at peace—as white is the highest spiritual color. The elevator symbolized consciousness, or awareness. The right side of the elevator referred to the right side, or spiritual side, of the brain. The elevator ascending signified a journey through the levels of consciousness. The blue light surrounding the evolved energy indicated a master teacher or spirit guide. I had experienced a changing of the guides, I believed, and a new spirit guide was now assisting me to grow to a higher spiritual level.

What a gift, I thought. I ended my dream entry by thanking the universe for such a wonderful experience.

Earlier that evening I had wondered if pets were delayed in their transition to the spirit world, because I had heard that some human spirits became earthbound as ghosts. This was the first time I had lost a pet, and I really wanted to know if Cashmere had made it. These dream revelations were my answers and reward for allowing myself to grieve and let go. I quietly fell back asleep.

From that point, I noticed more "coincidences." I felt as if a light switch had been turned on inside an extrasensory room in my mind. I didn't know yet, but that instructive dream from Cashmere would start me on an amazing journey, punctuated by an astrological event. The divine secrets revealed to me were incredible. Unbelievable experiences presented themselves. This was the beginning of my true spiritual awakening. I didn't yet know how tough this voyage would be or how active the afterlife had become.

At the age of five, I witnessed a séance held by my maternal grandmother. Our regular babysitter was not available, so I had to attend.

Mother told my sister, Alexis, my cousin Dean, and me to sit still in a corner of the room while the séance took place. Grandmother lit a cigar that smelled awful and a tall yellow saint's candle. Next, she placed a glass of water in front of her. Someone turned off the lights, and she started speaking in Spanish, which I did not understand, in an imploring tone, inviting whatever spirit she was seeking to contact.

Suddenly my aunt Nancy screamed, "Oh my God!" and fell off her chair onto the cold floor. The Spanish that had buzzed around the room among the family members abruptly stopped.

I froze on the hard chair in the dark room. I had no idea what was going on. There I was, almost scared out of my pants. Indeed, I was ready to wet them, especially when I heard the howling wind from an early winter storm, as it was a cold evening in New Jersey in December 1973.

Intuitively, I felt the spirits would speak through Grandmother. However, one must have come through Aunt Nancy. I stared at her body curled up in the fetal position on the floor, gasping for air as if a spirit had choked her. Suddenly she rose from the floor like a ghost and sat in her chair again as if nothing had happened. I was amazed that nobody reacted to her and wondered if everybody was in a trance. I wanted to help Aunt Nancy but was afraid to move.

Grandmother gestured with both hands in a slow, circular motion. I would later learn that this movement was designed to lower the vibration of energy in the room. "*Completa!*" she intoned, ending the ceremony.

Someone turned on the lights, and the room looked normal again, if heavy oak furniture crowded into every square inch can be called normal. Indeed, in every room in Grandmother's house, furniture had to be stepped over carefully, and no one could touch the ugly brown paneling or the smoke-covered paintings that covered the walls like a layer of cheap wallpaper.

Today, that experience seems a crucial part of my destiny—I was fated to be there at five years old to witness Grandmother's connection to the spirit world, not yet knowing how strongly the spirit world would subsequently affect my life. My dream state later became a conduit for spirit communication. More on this later.

I didn't think about the séance again until I spoke with Aunt Nancy many years later. She told me that Grandmother was a powerful medium who communicated with spirit guides and often lit a cigar and let it burn in an ashtray during the ceremony because one of her spirit guides enjoyed them.

The séance left a vivid imprint that my five-year-old brain stored away forever. In a recent meditative state, snapshots of my life experiences suddenly and swiftly flashed by like double-exposed photographs of a buried past through my mind's eye.

An early memory surfaced, showing me at the age of two and a half. The photo became a video, and I was running down the hallway of my grandparents' house. I stopped suddenly in the open space that bridged the living and dining areas, and my stomach sank. I looked around the empty room and sensed hostile energy surrounding me.

"Oh crap! Here I am again!" I said to myself and dropped a load in my diaper.

My inner voice responded, "Welcome to another earthly incarnation, Martin."

I had known I was reincarnated before I could comprehend the meaning. Between the ages of five and seven, I had recurring nightmares that my neighborhood was being invaded. I would hear tanks and bombs, which frightened me. I would often hide in the closet and put garbage bags full of clothes on top of me so the invaders wouldn't find me. Then I would wake up. I was finally relieved when these awful dreams stopped.

The age of eight was meaningful. Mother and her family (parents and four siblings) became estranged over a financial disagreement that year. I had never felt comfortable around them and, quite frankly, didn't miss them. My grandparents emigrated from Puerto Rico in 1950 and only spoke Spanish, and since I was never taught the language, I hardly communicated with them. My grandmother often snarled at me. My grandfather was mostly absent, only surfacing from the basement to eat. I had three uncles but saw only one of them regularly. I only had a relationship with my aunt Nancy and her son, my cousin Dean. But my relationship with Aunt Nancy soured the last year we were in contact, and the only member of this side of the family I did miss and thought about occasionally was my cousin Dean.

My parents divorced harshly when I was a toddler, and I had no conscious memories of my father. I knew only that he was eighteen years older than my mother. My household consisted of my mom, sister, and me, so I was elated at the thought of meeting my father for the "first" time at the age of eight. I wondered what he was like.

One spring afternoon, Mother arranged for me to finally see my father. We met at my grandparents' house before the estrangement, and he immediately hugged and kissed Alexis and me, filling me with indescribable joy!

Alexis and I sat on his lap for the next hour; I on the right side, Alexis on the left. I stared at his face—the white hair on the side of his head, the wrinkles on his forehead, and his beautiful brown eyes. As we sat and talked, he leaned over a couple of times and kissed my eyelid. It is one thing to kiss someone on the cheek, lips, or forehead, but a kiss on the eyelid was a new sensation. It left an imprint. I had craved a father's affection, and it felt great to finally receive it. It was a magical and loving memory.

After that day, I was a different boy. For a week, I felt like I was walking on clouds. I'd fallen in love with my daddy and desperately looked forward to seeing him again. I could not remember if we had made definite plans to meet, but I felt optimistic. Even as the weeks went by without a word from Father, I lived in a constant state of euphoria. I had a father!

I finished that school year on a high note and looked forward to the summer. I'd made some friends and had started playing sports.

Mother got the itch to move again. She told us to pack up because she had found an apartment around the corner from her family. This move would be different from the others because Alexis and I would change schools as well, this time attending Catholic school for the first time. We'd have to wear uniforms and enter a new world.

The first few days of Catholic school were uneventful. Besides the uniforms, I couldn't make out a distinction from public school, especially in academics. The principal was a tall, unattractive nun with a perpetually angry face. She walked the halls carrying a wooden paddle. On its side was a picture of a child getting spanked and the words "Board of Education" printed underneath.

I'd expected to see more nuns and priests teaching, but this was the mid-1970s, and Catholic schools were changing faculty members from clergy to civilians.

Just as the semester started, I attended my first funeral mass. My classmate Calvin's father had died unexpectedly. I sat in the pew at the back of the church, on the aisle, where I had an unobstructed view of the mass. The church filled with my schoolmates and Calvin's family and friends.

The service was long, and everybody in attendance received communion, which took up about half the ceremony. I sat looking around the church, inhaling the musty odors of wood and stone, wondering what happened to people when they died.

Finally the mass was over. The priest recited the closing prayer, and the organ played.

Calvin's family got up first. Some of the men picked up the casket and turned down the aisle to exit the church. As they approached my seat, I saw Calvin walking slowly behind his father's casket, staring straight ahead. Our teacher happened to be sitting in the next row, and I overheard her say to another teacher, "It hasn't hit him yet." I wondered what that meant. I hadn't yet been involved with the subject of death, and those words touched me deeply. It would be many years before I'd learn what that statement and the word *healing* meant.

Some weeks later Mother announced that Father wanted to see us again. I was thrilled. As each day passed, I looked forward to hugging and kissing him again. But sadly, that meeting never occurred. Something happened on the very day our meeting was scheduled. My mother hung up the phone and, without explaining why, told me we were not going to see Father after all.

I was crushed. I walked into my bedroom, stood in front of a mirror, looked into my sad eyes, and said, "I have a broken heart." For a long time after that, I walked around in pain, as if my heart literally hurt. I never saw my father again.

The following spring, I dressed in a suit for my first communion. Before we left for the church, Mother gave me a statue of a saint as my gift. She told me it was Saint Martin de Porres, patron saint of charity, the needy, and animals and that I had been named after him. I thought it was cool to be named after a saint, and I placed the statue on top of my dresser.

In the next few years, we moved from one roach-infested apartment to the next, and I continued to attend Catholic school. As an altar boy, I volunteered often to serve funerals when the church asked, since death fascinated me, but I still questioned what really happened to the soul.

During one cold Saturday morning in December, I woke to a quiet house. Alexis was asleep, and my mother was not in her bed. It looked like she had never come home from a night out with her friends since the bed was still made. I calmly ate a bowl of cereal, watched television, and waited until Alexis woke up.

About an hour later I received a phone call from Cassandra, one of the Cub Scouts' den mothers. She informed me that Mother had been involved in a car accident the night before. She'd had surgery that morning to repair a broken leg and was out of recovery."

My heart stopped. Cassandra continued in a calming voice, "Please wake up Alexis and tell her the news. Your mother has asked to see you and Alexis, so try to be dressed by noon, and I'll drive you to visit your mother at the hospital."

I sat quietly in Cassandra's car during the hour-long drive to the hospital, worrying how Alexis and I would cope with Mother in the hospital. After all, I had no relatives I could reach out to. So I prayed to God and asked that he take care of us until Mother came home. I walked into the hospital room and saw Mother's left leg elevated and in a cast from her thigh to her ankle. When she smiled, I noticed her front teeth were missing. "They were knocked out by the steering wheel from the impact of the accident," she said, and then she started to cry. "These are tears of joy. I am happy to be alive, and extremely grateful that Cassandra bought you here to visit me." Mother told us she had been driving, and her friend Cindy, a passenger in her car, had suffered minor injuries. Alexis and I slept at a neighbor's house the following week until Mother was released from the hospital.

The weeks that followed her release were rough. Only twelve and eleven, Alexis and I had to get ourselves to school, do our homework, and do *all* the housework. The neighbors occasionally blessed us with bags of groceries. Mother didn't have long-term disability insurance from her job, and since she had to be home for a few months, she had to borrow money from others. We also had to go on welfare to survive. When the holidays arrived, a neighbor delivered a Christmas tree to our apartment. Alexis and I enjoyed decorating it. The Catholic school donated wrapped Christmas gifts so Alexis and I could have presents to unwrap.

I turned to the church, my only spiritual outlet, for consolation and safety. New Year's arrived, and I made a promise to God that I would attend church daily so Mother's broken leg would heal. The church was only one block away, and I attended the 7:30 mass in the evenings—*religiously*. Even during the summer, when I played kickball with neighborhood kids, I stopped every night to attend mass. I wanted to keep my promise, and I did. Incredibly, I did not miss a single day of church that year. Mother's leg healed, and she returned to work. Shortly thereafter, she got a new job that paid more money, and we went off welfare the following year. I thanked God for answering my prayers and grew stronger spiritually.

I loved being an altar boy, especially serving weddings and funerals, because I got paid for these. The cash I received paid my dues for the sports and various clubs I participated in. If I had extra money, I bought ice cream from the Mr. Softee truck that frequented my block in the summertime.

One day after our monthly altar-boy meeting, Father Harry approached me privately and said, "You are an excellent altar boy. Would you be interested going on a day-long road trip to a monastery?" Since I loved being an altar boy, I agreed to the trip and looked forward to the experience.

The trip was on a Saturday. I was the lone altar boy accompanied by two priests in a grey van. During the three-hour ride, I didn't converse much, but I enjoyed the scenery. It was the first time I'd ever seen the country.

Toward the end of the drive, the van pulled off the highway, followed a curved road, made a sharp right turn, and climbed a hill. I saw acres of neatly manicured green grass. The land looked like a beautiful countryside postcard—the expansive landscape filled with colorful flowers, huge oak trees, and a giant building that looked like a castle atop the hill. The priest driving the van announced that we had arrived.

We exited the van and were met by another priest at the entrance. "Welcome! I hope you enjoyed your ride. Let me give you a tour."

From the outside, the building looked like a castle, but the inside was a different story. The first room I entered was the library. "If you study to become a priest, this is the room where you will read the Bible and pray," the priest stated with pride. "The next room is where you will meditate."

When I entered the sleeping quarters, I was amazed to see such a small bedroom. It held a small bed, a table, a lamp, a window, and a closet. It looked sad, and I didn't know if that was due to lack of natural sunlight, which was blocked by black drapes, or the dark paneling on the walls that framed this tiny resting area. I started feeling sleepy because the room looked so tired. A priest lived a life of austerity; there was nothing lavish about it.

For lunch we ate tuna fish sandwiches and canned soup. We sat on plastic chairs outside the kitchen area, directly behind the entrance to the building. I stopped and gazed at the beauty, peace, and tranquility of nature surrounding us. It was a vision I'd never forget.

After lunch we headed back home. The tour-guide priest shook my hand and gave me a warm salutation. On the trip home, all of us were quiet except for the priest in the passenger seat; he fell asleep sitting up and snored the whole way. I gazed out the window and contemplated the possibility of becoming a priest.

At the next altar-boy meeting, Father Harry asked if three of us kids would volunteer to assist the nuns at the convent with their grocery shopping that night. Without hesitation, I volunteered. I didn't have sports practice scheduled that evening and didn't want to stay home.

I entered another gray van with two other altar boys and one nun, Sister Lorraine, and wondered if the church issued only gray vans to its clergy.

At the grocery store, each altar boy was ordered to steer a shopping cart. After what seemed like hours, we'd filled our carts to capacity. I could not believe the amount of food we had. I could barely push the cart to the checkout counter; in fact, I said a Hail Mary prayer for the strength to push it.

We loaded the van with many bags of food and headed to the convent. Once we arrived, Sister Lorraine first guided us to the food cellar located in the basement. I was amazed at the size of this area: it spanned the entire length of the convent and had many aisles and shelves stacked with food. One entire aisle was dedicated to desserts. The basement looked like a mini grocery store.

Once we unloaded all the bags, we had to unpack all the items and store them in the proper aisles. I felt like I'd walked a mile sorting the items. The whole experience exhausted me. But by this point, I'd had a good look at how priests and nuns lived and thought it was a pretty peaceful lifestyle.

Another school season ended. My mother, who had been working as a bookkeeper for the Boy Scouts of America, informed me that she'd received a discount for sending me to Boy Scouts summer camp in Pennsylvania. I wasn't thrilled at the idea of going away to camp without any of my friends, especially since Pennsylvania seemed so far away from home. But as usual, my mother did not consider my feelings, so off to summer camp I went.

Far from the comforts of home and my routine with the church, I looked for spiritual comfort in the natural environment around me. I learned about animals that lived in the wild. I saw a bear, porcupine, and raccoon for the first time. I even learned how to pick up snakes and frogs. On one such occasion, while waiting to use the outside bathroom, I heard something squeaking and located a frog halfway in a snake's mouth. I immediately picked up the snake, opened its mouth, and allowed the still-intact frog to hop away to safety. I later learned that snakes eat frogs, and I felt sorry that the snake's hard work had been for naught, but I was glad to have saved the frog's life.

As I moved through adolescence, humor helped ease my passage and helped me escape. I had always been somewhat of a clown during school time. I sought attention or love by doing things to make others laugh, including myself. Toward the end of my eighth grade, on what must have been a full moon because the whole class was acting up, I was especially rambunctious. I must have said something that upset our substitute teacher, Sister Joan, a rare nun, hard and dry, desperate to control the adolescents under her care. Before I could even figure out what I'd said wrong, Sister Joan made a beeline to my seat.

She grabbed me by my tie and collar and lifted me out of my seat. She pulled me into her face and screamed, "If you don't shut up, I will kill you with my bare hands!" The whole class fell silent. I looked into her dilated blue eyes and saw absolute anger.

When she finally let go, I collapsed into my chair. Newly energized, she walked back to her desk and ordered the class to read a chapter from a book. I sat still and glanced often at her, still in disbelief of her threat. After school my classmates confessed their shock at Sister Joan's behavior. Fortunately, I never encountered Sister Joan after that day.

I was not fulfilled attending Catholic school, and needless to say, that experience did not bring me closer to God or answer questions about the reason we are on earth or if there's really is a heaven. I no longer desired to be a priest and looked forward to graduating and attending public high school.

Mother desired a better life and moved us from New Jersey to New York when I was fourteen years old. Alexis and I attended public high school and moved three more times during the next four years. We struggled financially and suffered an embarrassing eviction during this four-year stretch. I was elated to finally graduate in 1986.

Cashmere, the Siamese family cat, woke me up meowing for food on the morning of my eighteenth birthday. I thought about how well she had acclimated to three different homes during the first three years of her life. I looked in the mirror and sang "Happy Birthday" to myself. I was glad to finally be considered a legal adult. I also had a job interview on Wall Street for a full-time position at a brokerage firm. I had a good feeling that I would get that job, because it was my birthday.

The interview went well, and I was offered the job the following week. After being fingerprinted and passing a polygraph test, I became a stock-and-bond clerk. Whenever a client placed an order to sell in the stock market, it was my job was to obtain a specific stock or bond from a huge vault in a secure area. I then had to make sure the "security" (stock or bond) was properly registered and endorsed before it was deemed negotiable to transfer in the market. The company also offered tuition reimbursement if I attended college part-time and enrolled in business-related courses.

I adjusted to my daily nine-to-five working schedule and volunteered to work overtime to help my mother with living expenses. When Christmastime arrived, I received a $4,500 holiday bonus. I was thrilled. I immediately took driving lessons, passed my road test, and purchased a used car. It felt great to be more independent.

When the holidays passed, Mother got the itch to move again. I had decided the year before that my next domestic relocation would be to my very own apartment. The thought of venturing out on my own was both exciting and frightening. Mother had divorced at the age of twenty-two and had struggled to raise my sister and me as a single mother. We'd moved ten times in eighteen years as Mother continued her attempt to improve our living circumstances. But moving so often left me with a feeling of instability that I desperately wanted to change.

I knew my Christmas bonus would give me the financial boost I needed to live on my own. I was nineteen, but felt much older and more independent than my peers. I shared my intent with Alexis, who had moved out the year before. She supported the move and told me that her friend Lisa's mom, Betty, had just purchased a new home and wanted to rent out the studio apartment that came with the property. I felt elated with this opportunity.

That night I lay in bed and envisioned living in my own place and playing basketball in the backyard. I prayed to God to assist me in this move, and I fell asleep. I contacted Betty the following day and met with her after work. She showed me the apartment: a four-hundred-square-foot room and separate full kitchen and full bathroom. I left a small deposit and signed an agreement. I felt relieved. On my drive back home, I thanked God for answering my prayers. I told my mother that I had resolved to venture out on my own. She was surprised at first but then decided to start looking for an apartment for herself.

I created a budget and estimated my expenses. I realized that my small clerk's salary would mean I'd have to live paycheck to paycheck, but I didn't mind. Knowing I could live in a stable environment was priceless. Finally I could take charge of my life. I looked forward to the move and the new chapter of freedom.

Moving day finally arrived, and after unloading all my boxes, I enjoyed my first night in my Staten Island apartment. I slept well and went to work the next day. My focus was now on finding time to attend college and to go back to church, since I hadn't attended in years and felt lost spiritually, but first I had to confront a secret that had started to develop a stressful life of its own.

CHAPTER TWO

FREEDOM

My bed was a six-inch mattress in a pull-out couch. When folded up, it served as both my living-room sofa and dining chair. I ate dinner there, using an orange foam boogie board on my lap as a table. It took me a year to afford cheap paintings to dress up the stark white walls.

Betty was an angel. She was like a foster mom, and I felt more like a member of her family than a renter. She had cemented most of the grassy backyard except for a small area around the perimeter for growing vegetables and spices, so when the cement dried, I envisioned a basketball hoop hanging off the back deck. To my glee, Betty purchased a basketball hoop as a surprise for my twentieth birthday. I installed it that day and played basketball all afternoon. Later that evening I realized that my vision of living in my own apartment and playing basketball in the backyard had come true in less than a year. I realized with a chill that what I had envisioned had become manifest in physical form. Without consciously trying, I was beginning to realize the power of visualization.

The summer weekends were quiet, and my inner life had begun to clamor for attention. One evening while I watched a movie, I felt a bomb start to tick inside. I had a strong feeling that I had to confront a pressing issue buried within me before my feelings exploded. This bomb was my sexual orientation. I had always been physically attracted to men, but I had been uncomfortable expressing it.

I didn't have many friends and was a bit of a loner. Weekends were particularly lonely, and I had a lot of unanswered questions, so to deal with my inner turmoil, I took long evening drives to the New Jersey Shore listening to comforting music from the '50s and '60s. Most if not all of the songs were about the longing for love and the healing of an anguished heart. The music spoke to my soul. I desperately wished I had a father or grandfather I could talk to. I needed a male figure that could mentor me on life choices. After driving for many hours, my mind was tired and exhausted from contemplation. I had always been drawn to water and found the ocean and beaches spiritually rejuvenating. Those therapeutic drives quieted the torment in my heart and helped me sleep soundly.

I usually loved baseball season, but if the New York Yankees were not in the playoffs or World Series, I directed my attention to basketball. However, as I struggled with my sexuality, sporting events no longer saved me from the world or my life. I started suffering from insomnia. I feared rejection but knew that I needed to liberate myself with the truth.

Alexis and I built a relationship as young adults, and I felt secure around her. She introduced me to the wonderful topic of astrology, and we would speak for hours about it. I resolved to tell my family about my sexuality first, and then hopefully I'd find the support and confidence to tell my friends.

I called Alexis and said, "Since we all live separately now and get along better with each other, perhaps we could have a family dinner?"

Alexis, a sensitive and psychic Pisces, picked up a strong vibe that I needed to reveal something important. She organized a family dinner at her apartment for the following week.

Alexis cooked a great dinner of seafood pasta and salad greens. As I helped clean off the table, Alexis watched my behavior. She seemed to feel it was time to set the stage for me. Mother had turned on the TV to see one of her favorite shows, so Alexis muted it and proclaimed, "Marty has something he wants to tell us."

The room went silent. Mother looked bewildered. Alexis waited patiently, leaning her hands on one of the dining room chairs.

Unrehearsed, I blurted out, "I'm homosexual!" I started to cry.

Alexis said, "I knew it."

Mother rushed over saying, "You're not gay. You are going through a phase. Don't worry about it." Her eyes welled up, and she squeezed my hand tightly. "You're not gay. You're not gay." She repeated it as if to convince herself.

I felt so vulnerable that I did not want to be in her presence. I needed a supportive and compassionate person at this juncture—not an unaware and controlling mother. I excused myself and went to the bathroom for a moment of sanity. When I returned, Alexis was serving dessert, and my mother had gone back to watching her TV show. Things appeared normal, but I sat and thought about how weird everything felt. *Is everybody in shock, or are they going on with life?* I wondered. I really didn't know what else to expect, so I ate dessert and acted as if nothing out of the ordinary had happened. The night ended, and we went home.

The next day, I came across the page in my journal that had predicted my family's reaction. It was completely accurate. It confirmed that I was in close touch with my feelings and gave me the confidence to keep trusting myself. I felt vulnerable because I had just entered uncharted waters; by living more authentically and reclaiming my thoughts and feelings, I hoped my intuition would guide me.

The first holidays in my apartment were great. I felt proud as I decorated my little Christmas tree. In the evenings I turned off the lights and sat on the couch and watched the blinking tree lights. I was in a festive mood and grateful to have survived my first year on my own. I used my Christmas bonus to purchase gifts for family and friends, and I treated myself to cable TV. Now I could finally watch the New York Knicks basketball team instead of hearing them on the radio.

Around Easter, the company I worked for was being investigated for financial fraud. The scandal froze the company's assets, and employees were laid off. Rumors buzzed around Wall Street that the company would go out of business, and employees panicked. Headhunters—people who worked for job-placement agencies—called daily to place employees at other financial institutions. My manager informed me that if a job opportunity surfaced, I should pursue it aggressively. A week later a headhunter called me with a job opportunity at a bank. I faxed my updated resume to the recruiter and awaited a call to schedule an interview.

The recruiter contacted me a few days later with the interview date, time, and location. The job description was similar to my current position, but the salary was 50 percent greater. The only drawback was that the bank didn't issue year-end holiday bonuses. However, I knew that a higher steady income would afford me a better lifestyle, so I was motivated to land this new job.

On the day of the interview, I entered the lobby of the bank and had a strong instinct that I would be employed there. The lobby felt very familiar, even though I had never entered it before. The interviewer was pleasant, and I left the bank feeling optimistic. It took six more weeks and two additional interviews before I was offered the job. I handed in my two-week resignation notice to my current employer and prepared for my new position.

By now, the novelty of coming out of the closet had worn off. I was glad that my professional life had reached another rung, but my personal life felt stagnant. I hadn't had a serious relationship and longed for an intimate union. I was also still closeted with my friends. Another lonely summer arrived, and I felt sad again.

This time, instead of falling into a depression, I made the choice to seek a therapist on my own. During my first session, the therapist asked me a thought-provoking question: "How do you react when something troubles you?"

His question unlocked my unconscious limiting beliefs, and I realized something for the first time. I answered, "I withdraw and isolate myself for protection instead of reaching out and expressing my feelings. Even though I've mustered the courage to come out to family members, I reverted to isolation out of fear. It sort of happened without me knowing." As I spoke, I realized how easily unconscious behaviors, especially unhealthy ones, would creep back into my life unless I consciously reprogrammed my subconscious. I also realized that bottling up emotions was toxic.

I felt empowered by the session. After two months of weekly sessions, I had the courage to attend a gay social group where I could express my feelings openly. I also started journaling my thoughts every day instead of occasionally. I came to the realization that I needed to open up, trust my friends, and face the illusion or fear of rejection in order to feel loved. I finally came out to all my friends. They all admitted that they had suspected anyway, and they embraced me even more. I learned that by accepting myself, I had found the key to happiness. By the end of the summer, I had gained the courage to place a personal ad and start dating.

I continued my path of healing and growing by returning to church, attending weekly as I had when I was younger. I also enrolled at a local college and studied two business courses. My high school friends Dave and Carla got married that summer, and I was an usher at their wedding. Theirs was the first wedding I had ever attended, and to be involved in it was magical. I enjoyed the atmosphere of celebration and love that united everyone at the wedding. I realized that, gay or straight, love was all that mattered.

The first few months on the new job were hectic. Learning a new company policy took time, and I had a lot of responsibility, but I excelled in my new position. I met pleasant people and befriended Evelyn, an attractive African American woman who was old enough to be my mother but who looked my age. She was a kindred spirit whom I trusted and shared everything with. We often spoke for many hours about meaningful topics such as childhood issues, spirituality, and relationships.

I was invited to a friend's New Year's party that featured a locally prominent psychic named Pearl. Pearl was seated in the back room, separated from the rest of the guests. I had never experienced a psychic reading but had always been curious about it. I placed my name on the reading list and waited for my turn.

When my turn arrived, I entered the room and saw a short lady in her late sixties with a wrinkled face and gnarled fingers shuffling a deck of regular playing cards. When I made eye contact, I felt her gaze penetrate me.

"Come over and sit down," she said in a raspy voice. "Smile; this is not going to hurt."

She looked me over and smiled. "You are lonely. I know someone who could befriend you. He's a good friend of mine. He's a little older than you, but I feel he could mentor you. Would you like to meet him?"

"Sure," I replied.

"Here, write down your phone number, and I'll have him call you. His name is Ted."

This psychic is good, I thought. *How did she know I'm gay?* She captivated my attention for the rest of the evening."

"Do you see your father often?" she asked.

"No, I'm estranged from him. Is he still alive?"

"Yes, he thinks of you a lot. He lives in Texas. You can find him if you want to look for him. You will get a promotion and a good raise this summer," she continued. "I see steady income for you. You have only good friends—no enemies." She smiled.

The rest of my reading inspired and energized me. I thanked and paid her and then returned to the party.

Ted called the next day. He introduced himself and said he was a friend of Pearl's. I could tell from the vibration of his voice that he was a kind and honest person. We chatted briefly and found out we worked a few blocks away from each other. We decided to meet for lunch the following week.

When we met, Ted walked up to me and shook my hand. I looked into his eyes and instantly knew he was a kind soul. He was a handsome, six-foot-tall man in his midthirties. Our lunch meeting was great; we connected on a spiritual level. We made plans to have dinner that weekend.

During dinner, Ted spoke candidly about his life experiences, sharing both his saddest and happiest moments. Ted was ten years older than me, and being very impressionable, I listened to every detail of his wisdom. He said that every obstacle or loss he'd endured had made him stronger. I felted blessed to encounter such an honest person. I valued his testimony, and we began what would become an enduring friendship. My plea for a mentor had been answered!

Alexis had moved to Queens, New York, the year before. As adults we'd started to communicate more and become closer. We became engulfed in the subject of astrology as a focus to deal with our family issues. I read many books on the subject, especially during the summer after my college finals. While canvassing the local bookstore one day, I came across the self-help section and picked up a book titled *The Power of Positive Thinking* by Norman Vincent Peale. I opened it to a random page and read, "Your thoughts create your reality." That seemed plausible, since a thought had manifested my apartment. I read a few more pages and decided to purchase it.

The book transformed my mind. I became more conscious of my thoughts and learned how to think more positively. I realized that I didn't have to think or act negatively or blame anybody for my problems. In fact, I learned, if I thought of an obstacle as a problem, then it became one. This was a huge revelation for me.

After completing my spring semester, I vacationed in Florida to destress from finals and my full time job. Having worked a few years in the financial industry, I knew it was not a career that would fulfill me in the long term. As I rested on the beach, I searched for my heart's desire. I needed my present job and income, so making a drastic career change now wasn't realistic. I tried to imagine what would be fun—what I really desired to do. An image of cooking surfaced in my mind. I loved to cook and knew I would excel in culinary school. So without hesitation, I decided to follow my intuition and trust its power.

Back in New York, I chose not to enroll for the fall semester at the college I'd previously attended. Instead I enrolled in a culinary school that had a part-time curriculum and affordability. Since the culinary courses weren't related to business, I couldn't obtain reimbursement for my expenses; I had to pay for them it was all out-of-pocket. So I applied and qualified for a student loan through the school and obtained a personal loan from my employer for the rest of the tuition. I looked forward to becoming a certified chef.

Orientation at the culinary school was fun. We purchased our cooking uniforms, school utensils, and sophisticated knife kits. I met many students, ranging from high school age to retirees. Many of them were changing careers to pursue the culinary arts.

As my culinary education started, my first intimate relationship with a gentleman named Rodger ended. He was a handsome medical student whom I'd met through a personal ad. The courtship had lasted only a few months, but it was the first time I'd fallen in love, and I was crushed. I felt deep emotional pain and shed many tears for many days. It was a horrible and painful experience.

Alexis was instrumental in my healing. She gave me a book called *How to Survive the Loss of a Love* by Bloomfield, Colgrove, and McWilliams. The book taught me the three stages of recovery (shock and denial, anger and depression, understanding and acceptance). I hadn't known there were stages for healing, and it was extremely comforting to know that I'd survive the pain. Alexis said the book had helped her heal from her first heartbreak. That book was glued to my hip for the next few months. I learned what it was to feel emotional pain but, more important, how to heal.

As I slowly got over Rodger, My classmate Eli and I developed a friendship. He and I would walk outside during our fifteen-minute break from cooking in the hot kitchen. He'd noticed that I seemed sad and asked me why. I told him I was grieving from a breakup. He then opened up and shared that he'd gone through a breakup two weeks before and was still hurting. When he revealed he was gay, I did the same—and our friendship cemented. We would grab a quick drink and share our grief at a local bar after school. I thanked God for guiding me to a wonderful friend and someone to heal with.

Meanwhile, I turned twenty-three, and my Wall Street job became more stressful. My company had laid off 15 percent of the staff, and the resulting workload overwhelmed me. I had to work on Saturdays to catch up. Sunday was homework day, so I had no leisure time left. To make matters worse, my car's engine died, and I was told it wasn't worth fixing. Unfortunately I couldn't afford another used car, so I decided to junk the old one and rely on public transportation instead. It was a rough summer: a stressful job, culinary school, no car, and tight funds—all while trying to heal from a broken heart.

I focused on music to get me through the year. I listened to it while traveling to and from work and school. Slowly, I stopped crying and started laughing more. I no longer dwelled obsessively on Rodger or the breakup. I learned that letting go was liberating. I felt vulnerable but free. I'd learned that holding on to Rodger or the illusion of the relationship made me sad. I understood that those who had jaded opinions of their ex-lovers had not let go of them. I started to feel good about me—whoever I was. I also wrote many small notes of inspiration to myself whenever I felt inundated with stress. These daily affirmations got me through the rough times.

The day after Christmas, I wrote a note to myself for the upcoming year and hung it in my office. It said, "1992 is, and will be, an absolute dedication year for me. Simplicity in every form will be established in my life." I dated, timed, and signed the note. It was my new focus, and I was going to make sure it happened.

With just one week left to graduate, I had to find time to memorize and practice cooking twenty different recipes for my final exam. Even though the exam called for only two recipes, none of the students knew which two we'd learned that semester that we had to perfect. We were graded on preparation, cooking method, and presentation. The courses would be served to food critics seated in the restaurant. I only had time to shop, cook, and master ten of the recipes that week. I prayed to God, "Please make sure I get to cook the recipes that I have practiced."

The evening of my final exam arrived. The students were seated at a large round table in the restaurant. The head chef instructed us that he'd divided the twenty recipes across ten small sheets, containing two recipes each. He folded these sheets and placed them into a tall white chef's hat. He instructed us to approach him one at a time, and after the first student chose, students would proceed to choose according to their seating positions counter-clockwise around the table, and pick out one sheet for our finals.

I was the last to pick. When I pulled out the sheet and opened it, I could not believe my luck: not only had I picked two of the recipes I'd mastered, I picked out the same two recipes I'd practiced the night before, and they were my favorite to cook. I instinctively knew this was divinely guided. I aced the final exam.

Because the school had set a schedule for final exams, only four of us were taking our test that evening. Eli was in my group. Luckily, we all passed, so we went out and celebrate our completion. We headed to a jazz bar in the East Village and drank champagne. We listened to music and laughed all night. Eli and I were even more proud to have survived an emotional roller coaster of a year. I had learned the real meaning of fortitude that year.

Once my culinary studies were behind me, the spirit world entered my life.

CHAPTER THREE

VISITORS

My personal dedication year started off well with the exception of working many overtime hours. One company perk for working past eight was a ride home in a corporate taxi. On those rides home, I watched the bright lights of the fantastic city diminish and the skyscraper that I just occupied get smaller as I rode further away from Manhattan. After many long evenings, I often gazed out the window of the company car and wondered, *What is my contribution to the world? What are my soul's true purpose and my spiritual mission?* While I enjoyed cooking school, which temporarily fulfilled my creative desires, I still felt a longing that I could not yet identify.

I slept peacefully eight hours a night. I had only averaged five to six hours sleep the year before, so my body thanked me for the rest.

My responsibilities to pay for my living expenses and educational loans kept me at my bank job. I knew that once these loans were paid, I would be less burdened and free to make different choices. So I embraced the overtime and viewed it as an opportunity to also save more money for a used car.

I resurrected my social life once again. It was great to enjoy gatherings on weekends rather than homework and office work. My friendship with Carla and Dave, my old high school friends, grew stronger, and I also befriended Carla's friend Amy. We all went to the movies, the beach, bowling alleys, concerts, and sporting events.

One interesting day at work, while I walked by a clear glass cubicle, I made eye contact with a young man sitting behind a computer. I hadn't seen him before, so I figured he was probably a temporary employee filling in for someone on maternity leave or on vacation. His deep blue eyes captivated me. I felt no romantic interest, yet I felt drawn to him.

Later that same day, he walked by my desk to deliver some documents and introduced himself as Brock. We discussed the documents and then conversed about music and sports. He had just graduated from college, lived with his girlfriend, and was pursuing full-time employment. In our conversation, we found out that we were both huge basketball fans and loved the New York Knicks. We talked for twenty minutes about our similar interests before reluctantly getting back to work.

I arrived the next day to find a stack of CDs and a note from Brock on my desk. The note read: "Marty, Listen to these CDs to see if you like some of the alternative bands we discussed yesterday. Please take your time listening; there is no rush to return these."

I was touched by his gesture, so I walked to his office and thanked him personally. I listened to the music all week. We followed that year's basketball season together and became good friends.

Betty and her immediate family had become my extended family, so we gathered together during the holidays. Betty had remarried and her new husband, Marvin, was a humorous man who loved to play practical jokes on me frequently. Betty's aunt Millie, a native of Brooklyn, New York, who loved pizza, came to visit from her retirement community in Atlantic City, New Jersey. I adored her immensely. Betty's daughters, Lisa and Samantha, and my sister, Alexis, all came to celebrate Christmas as well. Since graduating from culinary school, I had cooked Christmas Eve dinner for everyone.

That year, three days after Christmas, Aunt Millie was suddenly hospitalized with chest pains. She passed away a few days later from a ruptured aorta. I was so sad to hear the news, and it put a damper on the New Year's celebration.

Several days after her funeral, I experienced a bizarre occurrence: I was watching TV around midnight one evening when my phone rang. I was startled since I usually didn't get calls that late at night. I answered it and heard static. I muted the TV and listened more closely. I heard a faint voice that sounded like Aunt Millie say, "I'm okay." I was shocked. I listened for another 30 seconds but heard only static. I then hung up and sat in silence with chills running through my body.

Did I just receive a phone call from heaven? I wondered. I thought about waking up Betty to tell her but decided not to. I wasn't sure if I believed that myself, and I seriously doubted that Betty would have believed me either. I figured that the message was for me, so I kept it a secret.

That year, the Knicks made the playoffs. Brock, another coworker, and I bought tickets for one of the playoff games held at the world's most famous arena, Madison Square Garden. We loved it. The Knicks won, and the crowd exploded! The energy was incredible. While exiting the arena, Brock and I filled out season-ticket requests in the hopes that one of us would be chosen. A few weeks later I was contacted by mail and offered two seats, so Brock and I became season-ticket holders.

Then Ted called me one evening to tell me that his friend Pearl, the psychic, had passed away. We made plans to attend her wake and go to dinner afterward. At the wake, I looked at Pearl's still body and saw only a shell. *She was not that body*, I thought. *Where did her spirit go*? *Is her spirit present here at the wake?* I knelt by her body, said a prayer for her peaceful soul, and silently thanked her for introducing me to Ted.

At dinner, Ted shared an emotional story: He had visited Pearl a couple of days before in the hospital. When he walked into the room, she opened her eyes and said, "Hi, Ted. I love you." He'd stopped in his tracks in shock. He said that his deceased mother's voice had come out of Pearl's mouth. Stunned, I listened to him with my mouth open. Ted's mother had passed away several years before while Ted was at work. He hadn't gotten get a chance to say good-bye or hear his mom's final words. After "Pearl's" statement, he welled up with emotion. He had intended to visit Pearl at the hospital and had received a gift from heaven, compliments of his mother.

Aunt Millie's call, Pearl's death, and Ted's experience prompted me to wonder again about what really happened when a person died. Although I had been drilled with hollow teachings about heaven and hell in Catholic school, I innately knew there was more to life after death. I questioned my motive for still attending services at the Catholic church. When I was growing up, attending mass had been mandatory at school, and now I felt it was an habit I performed unconsciously that didn't bring me any closer to God. In fact, I still didn't know who or what God was. I'd never bought into the theory that God was an old man staring at me from the corner of the ceiling, judging my every move. I asked friends why they attended church. The most popular answer I received was, "Because we're supposed to." It seemed like a lame answer. I needed something to believe and grow in, not something to conform to. I decided to stop attending church. I wanted to seek other means to satisfy my spiritual thirst. This one decision—consciously using my free will—opened my heart to spiritual truths that healed and liberated me. It became my mission to seek spiritual truth, and the universe heard me.

On a rare day off from work, I came across a program on TV called *The Other Side*. The show featured a medium named James Van Praagh, who had the gift to communicate with deceased loved ones in heaven or the spirit world. I watched as he provided true testimonies to a skeptical and grieving father who had just lost his young son. The father asked that James tell him the nickname he used to use for his son. James closed his eyes and telepathically encouraged the young boy in spirit to impress upon him the nickname. James then opened his eyes and blurted out, "Doctor! You called him doctor!" The rugged and stern-looking father smirked and nodded in agreement. I could almost see his heart start mending. I then watched a young man's heartfelt reaction when James confirmed that his deceased mother always knew he was gay: a "secret" that the son thought his mother never knew. I was captivated that James could talk to dead people. I became hungry to discover how life-after-death communication took place, so I watched James every time he appeared on TV.

At the age of twenty-five, I felt more peace come over me. I wanted to preserve this feeling forever. One evening as I lay down to go to sleep, I had an experience that deepened my spiritual interest. I lit my customary white tea-light candle to provide illumination for the angels who I believed protected me while I slept. I closed my eyes to pray, and a vision came to my mind's eye: A beautiful Caucasian woman appeared wearing a white-ruffled blouse, with her hair up in a bun. She had the most beautiful blue eyes and the warmest smile I'd ever witnessed. She emanated pure love. I opened my eyes and received the impression that this woman was a spirit guide. I thanked her for the visit and fell asleep thinking about her.

I woke up the next morning still thinking about the beautiful spirit. I didn't know it then, but I'd seen her through the eye of clairvoyance. I named her Blue Eyes and started to pay more attention to my visions.

The following spring was the best NBA season that the Knicks had experienced since they'd won the championship in the '70s. During the playoffs, the Knicks made it to the finals, only to lose in seven games to the Houston Rockets.

Winter proved fun that year. I took several weekend ski trips to upstate New York with friends. The view from mountaintops was spectacular. The mountains felt healing and were beautiful—I felt like I was inches away from heaven. My consciousness ascended each time I rode higher on the ski lift. I skied down different mountains to try out runs at various levels of difficulty. I learned that choice played a huge role in what slope I went down—as it did in choosing my path in life. I also learned that once I mastered a challenging slope, I was ready to tackle the next obstacle. That experience taught me about my adventurous side and about the adventurous side of life. I had never considered taking risks before; I had always focused my energies on finding safety and surviving.

Brock had found success at a full-time job at another company. Since we shared season tickets, we kept in touch and saw each other often during basketball season. He often spoke of his girlfriend and his mom, Molly, whom he adored. He also had an older brother, Luke, whom he rarely mentioned.

Brock never asked me about my personal life. He was the only person I hadn't told I was gay. We never had deep, meaningful discussions. Even after years of friendship and our sharing of season tickets, our friendship was limited to sports, music, and the financial industry. I desired a deeper bond and wanted to share my sexual orientation with him. It seemed that coming out of the closet was a never-ending process. I felt more stressed when I didn't share myself fully, so I decided to broach the subject with him at the beginning of the next basketball season.

When the season arrived, we met at a local sports bar to have our usual chicken wings and fries before the game. I asked him the typical questions, and he answered with his quick wit. His one-word answers made me feel a little uncomfortable. *Can we share deep discussions?* I wondered. Then I received a hunch that Brock's older brother, Luke, might be gay. The more I thought about it, the stronger my intuition felt. I broached the subject in a nonthreatening way.

"Is your brother married?" I asked.

"No."

"Is he gay?"

Brock looked surprised for a moment. "I don't know what he is."

Bingo! I used this opportunity to convey my truth. "Well, if your brother is gay, it's okay, because I date men."

Stunned, he stared into my eyes and listened quietly.

"There is nothing wrong with gay people," I continued. "They're normal, like anybody. You probably can't tell if someone is gay, because most of the time it's not obvious."

He nodded in agreement but didn't say anything else on the topic. We continued to watch the pregame show blaring from the TVs until we left for the arena. Once the game ended, we shook hands as usual and headed to our respective modes of transportation. On my bus ride back home, I was relieved that I'd conveyed my truth to Brock and was amazed that my intuition had been correct once again.

My love of sports led to another character-building experience. I enjoyed white-water rafting and eventually became the organizer for my company's yearly fall rafting trip. The group of us friends and coworkers car pooled on the 120-mile drive to the Delaware Water Gap. That year, we encountered stormy weather. The winds and rains delayed the twelve-mile trek down the river by two hours. The instructor told us the dam was open, and that it was creating more rapids. This made the adventure seem more exciting, but I knew it would also be more treacherous.

The river had rapids ranging from level one, with miniature waves, to level six, which involved huge rapids and would require a helmet, experience, and certification to navigate. Our group was scheduled for the intermediate level-three rapids. After the delay the instructor informed us that we might encounter level-four rapids due to the inclement weather. Another coworker and I were the most experienced rafters, so we were made captains. We traveled with five people to a raft: two front paddlers, two middle paddlers, and the captain in the back controlling the steering. We were confident that we would survive, so we put on our wetsuits and life vests, boarded the raft, and set off down the river.

The October foliage added beauty to the voyage. Most of us had a wonderful time, but the front paddlers on my raft, my friend Jackie and her boyfriend, fought all day long. Their discontent affected the raft's direction. As we approached the eight-mile marker, we saw tough rapids ahead. I relinquished my captain spot and swapped positions with Jackie, who was still fighting and paddling erratically. I almost paid for that choice with my life.

When we hit the rapids, we tried to maneuver around some huge rocks. Our raft bounced so high that waves of water flooded in. I instructed the middle two paddlers to stop paddling and bail out the raft in hopes of regaining some buoyancy. Water splashed everywhere; I had trouble seeing anything.

Within seconds I heard Jackie yell, "Let's hit the big rock!" The next thing I felt was my body going up in the air, flipping backwards, and hitting the churning forty-nine-degree water.

By the time I had risen to the surface, I had swallowed so much water that I couldn't catch my breath. I struggled to breathe as my body was pulled downriver. The life vest barely kept me afloat and didn't protect me from slamming into rocks. When I bobbed up for air, I caught a glimpse of one of my rafting mates clinging to life on a tree branch. I thought, *I'm glad he's holding a tree branch; he has two young boys, and I don't want him to die.*

Then a deep fatigue set in and my body slowed down. I no longer had the strength to panic or to struggle, so I looked up toward the cloudy sky and said, "God, I'm only twenty-seven. I cannot die yet."

Within seconds, Jackie's boyfriend grabbed me. He'd served as a marine, and his grip was strong as steel. He held me up as high as he could so I could breathe. Every tiny bit of air I gulped burned my lungs like fire. Jackie's boyfriend continued to hold me while we floated down the river until a tour guide paddled over on his kayak. He instructed me to hold on to the side of kayak until the other raft mates were rescued. It took all of my will to hold on as waves slammed into me. Somehow, we were all rescued, and none of us suffered major injuries. I thanked Jackie's boyfriend for saving my life.

The stress of the event gave me a headache that lasted for days; however, I was humbled to be alive and healthy. I felt like I'd been rescued by divine intervention.

After we returned to work, rumors flew around the office that our jobs were being relocated to Florida within the year. Workers panicked, and the office atmosphere quickly turned unhealthy. Stress and tension filled the air. Once the company confirmed the rumor, many felt anxious, and others displayed cavalier attitudes. The company announced that it would offer only a select few the option to relocate. This created a lot of uncertainty.

I finally paid off all of my loans and had already been looking forward to seeking other employment opportunities. I contacted friends who worked at other organizations to set up job interviews for me. I interviewed at three other organizations, and two offered me positions. I chose the job that paid more and agreed to take the company's mandatory drug test. A few days later the company told me I had passed the drug test and that they would fax me a written offer. Once I received this offer and agreed to the salary, I planned to submit my resignation to the bank.

The following morning I received the official job offer. I called to acknowledge it and scheduled an afternoon appointment with the human resources department to confirm the salary. An hour before my appointment, a senior manager from my current job called me into her office.

She closed the doors, placed a package in front of me, and said, "Congratulations, you have the option to relocate to the Florida office. The relocation package includes all expenses paid and a promotion. We will fly you and another down to Florida within the next two weeks so you can tour the city and decide. Here is the relocation contract. You have one month to accept or decline."

Filled with conflicting emotions, I walked back to my desk. Now I had two options to consider: moving to Florida or staying in New York. I kept my appointment with my new possible employer and mentioned the offer I had just received from my current employer. The human resources person understood my predicament and encouraged me to fully examine both possibilities. She even hinted that she would love to relocate to Florida if the opportunity ever presented itself. I thanked her for understanding and told her that I would make the decision within a week.

I turned to my astrological makeup to make this decision. My Cancer sun sign and Pisces moon sign gave me the intuition and divine insight to make the right decision. The more I thought about relocating, the happier I felt. By the third day, even though I had yet to experience the company tour of Florida, I had silently made up my mind to move.

My company scheduled a flight to Florida the following week. I took Alexis with me and fell in love with Tampa and the beautiful beaches in nearby St. Petersburg and Clearwater. During the van tour of a quaint shopping village, I noticed a restaurant with a yellow awning, not knowing that its significance would reveal itself to me a year later.

I returned to New York convinced that I had made the right decision. I contacted my other potential employer and told them about my decision to relocate. They wished me well and said that if I ever moved back to New York, I could contact them.

My company gave me five months' notice to relocate, which gave me ample time to say good-bye to close friends and acquaintances. The two things I would miss the most were Alexis and my Knicks season tickets. I gladly let go of everything else, including the studio apartment I had lived in for nine years. I had outgrown its space some years before but was glad to have lived there since it gave me the domestic security and stability that I craved. I was also happy to say good-bye to ten years of commuting to Wall Street and the cold winters.

I enjoyed my last summer in New York. My friend Judy and I spend most of the summer together. We had dated briefly in high school and eventually became great friends instead. I had a three-month farewell tour that included my ten-year high school reunion and many parties. I also attend a fundraiser and won an astrological report from the silent auction. I went to the metaphysical store a week later to claim my prize. The printed report described my birth chart and yearly transits, which confirmed a possible change in my domestic environment that year.

Betty's youngest daughter, Lisa, had married and relocated to Florida the year before. She called to say she was expecting a son and asked if I would be his godfather. I was honored and gladly accepted. My godson Matt was born a week before my birthday—another Cancer.

My company furnished me with real estate listings and contacts in Florida. They also provided a week of paid leave and travel expenses for my search. From my New York apartment, I had reviewed the apartment listings and the great amenities on offer. I was particularly drawn to a new waterfront apartment complex with a gated entrance, an indoor air-conditioned basketball court, and a view of Tampa Bay. After surviving nine New York summers with only a fan, I loved the idea of living in a place with air-conditioning. I prayed to God and asked that I be guided to a safe place in Florida.

I faxed a list of apartments to Valerie at the real estate office and flew to Florida the next week. When I arrived, Valerie had crossed off four of the ten apartments I'd selected, explaining that those apartments were not in great neighborhoods and that she didn't want me to waste my time looking there. I liked her attitude from the start and felt she was a savvy woman who knew what I was looking for and who had my best interest at heart.

We stopped at five apartment complexes the first day. I liked three of the five, including the waterfront complex I'd desperately wanted to see. Unfortunately there were no availabilities at any of those three. We ended our search and planned to resume the next day.

The next morning before we sought out possible new residences, Valerie strongly suggested that we add my name to waiting lists for the three apartment complexes we'd seen the day before. We visited the waterfront apartment first since that was the complex I loved the most. We sat in the clubhouse and waited until we were summoned into the office. Valerie advised the attendant that we'd been there the day before and that I wanted to put my name down on the waiting list. She also added that I would need the apartment by the beginning of September—only five weeks away.

I provided the attendant with my criteria for an apartment: one bedroom plus den and on the waterfront. The attendant suddenly stopped writing and said, "I believe a resident just broke their lease minutes ago. They just faxed their thirty-day notice to vacate, and I believe the apartment has the same criteria that you're looking for."

The attendant stepped away to read the faxed letter to confirm this information. She walked back in and said, "This must be your lucky day. A one-bedroom-plus-den waterfront apartment is going to be vacant, and I can see that no one is on the waiting list for that."

I couldn't believe my luck. Valerie immediately asked if we could see a model of the same type of apartment. The attendant agreed and took us on the tour. The apartment was beautiful. It had twelve-foot vaulted ceilings with crown molding and new carpeting. The bathroom was spacious and had a Roman tub. The walk-in closet was huge, the view of the bay was spectacular, and the price was affordable. I agreed to take the next availability and filled out the application. After my application and credit check were approved, I left a deposit.

I flew back to New York in awe that my prayers had been answered, and I felt that my move to Florida was the start of a new chapter although I was unaware that this move would initiate a new script. It was the real beginning of my spiritual awareness and my *true* education. Events fated to occur became manifest in my life.

CHAPTER FOUR

FATE

One month later I flew back to Florida on the eve of my godson Matt's baptism.

I reminisced about my closest friendships in New York and was amazed at how naturally they had formed. People had come into my life effortlessly, and we had shared many spiritual commonalities. I hoped that new friendships would form just as easily in Florida. I embraced this new beginning and looked forward to Matt's special day.

Just off the Interstate; I noticed a sign welcoming me to Martin County. *Interesting,* I thought. *That's my name.* Next, I took the exit to Stuart, Florida, and saw that the state route was 714—my birthday. As I neared Lisa's house, I looked forward to holding Matt in my arms for the first time. I was "Uncle" Marty to many of my friends' children, and I especially enjoyed holding and feeding babies.

Lisa and Greg welcomed me and handed me their firstborn, my godson, for the first time. Matt had huge blue eyes and loads of platinum-blond hair; he looked just like his attractive Irish mom. He seemed to trust me instantaneously when I looked into his eyes. He smiled often and hardly made a sound.

On Matt's christening day, the attendees met an hour prior for a photo session at Lisa's house. Then Alexis and I (the godparents), Lisa, Matt, and Greg carpooled to the church. When we pulled up in front, I did a double-take at the name: Saint Martin de Porres Church.

I looked at Lisa and said, "I had no idea Matt would be baptized in this church. I was named after this saint and didn't know they named a church after him." I also shared other "coincidences": Matt and I shared the same astrological sign of Cancer, and the county name and state route aligned with my life. All these signs led me to believe that these events had been scripted to occur—I was meant to be Matt's godfather.

A few days after the christening, I moved and settled into my beautiful waterfront apartment. After a lifetime of winters in New York, I especially enjoyed Florida's many sunny days.

But right after the New Year, my job sent me on a two-week business trip to London—right in the heart of a cold English winter. The flight had a stopover in New York. On the first leg of my trip, I sat next to a lieutenant commander of the New York City Police Department. He was flying back from Boulder, Colorado, after assisting in the JonBenét Ramsey murder case. He didn't share any details from that investigation but started an inspired and spiritual conversation about life.

He said, "I have a desire to assist people and will fly anywhere to lend my services to help others." He radiated a passion about his spiritual mission. He deplaned in New York while I stayed on to continue to London. Before he left the plane, he popped open his briefcase and handed me a plastic square plate the size of a bumper sticker. It read, "Remember, we work for God," and had his name and police title engraved in the bottom right corner. I thanked him with a strong handshake and kept the gift close. I knew I would keep it in my home office from then on.

On my flight to London, I thought about how happy the lieutenant had been feeling that he worked for God. I wanted to feel the same fulfillment in my vocation. My current job paid the bills, but the competitive, political environment did not nurture my soul.

In London, I quickly adapted to the Queen's English and the British habits. Every weekday at noon, my London counterparts headed to the pubs for a pint of beer to wash down their lunches. Since I was an inexperienced drinker, a true lightweight, I settled for only a half pint. My coworkers nicknamed me Half-Pint and called me that for the duration of my trip. It was my first trip overseas, and while it was rewarding in many ways, the cold and dreary weather wore on me. The sun only peeked through the clouds twice in twelve days. When I finally flew home, I was happy to be back in the warm sunshine and to sleep in my own bed again.

Soon after I returned, Brock called to say that he was flying down to Florida to visit his mom and brother and wanted to invite me over to dinner so I could meet them. They both lived in West Palm Beach, Florida, a four-hour drive from Tampa, so Brock invited me to stay overnight. I happily accepted his invitation.

Molly, Brock's mom, was a pretty lady with gorgeous blue eyes and short blonde hair. She was a wonderful host. During my visit, she showered me with attention and food and hugged me with open affection. Initially, Brock's brother Luke was reserved with me. He observed everything from a distance—a true Scorpio, the psychological detective. As the evening unfolded, he showed more of his sensitivity but remained guarded most of the time. He seemed to be a shy soul who absorbed more than he expressed. I knew he was gay and sensed that he was still uncomfortable with it. The four of us enjoyed a steak dinner, played a board game, and laughed late into the evening. Brock accompanied me when I drove Luke to his apartment. Luke barely said a word on the drive, but he smiled whenever Brock or I cracked a joke. After I dropped him off, I stayed overnight at Molly's and headed back home the next morning. My family circle had been extended.

That fall, two of my close friends got married on back-to-back weekends. I booked a ten-day visit to New York to accommodate both weddings and also scheduled an appointment with an astrologer named Bob Marks, whom an ex-coworker had highly recommended. I had read a few astrology books and won a printed report of my birth chart, but I had never been to a professional astrologer and looked forward to the experience.

I already knew that the birth chart was a snapshot of the solar system at the exact time in the location of birth, showing the planets' placements at a specific degree in a specific zodiac sign and providing a spiritual blueprint for this incarnation. But I couldn't believe the accuracy of the testimony the astrologer provided just by looking at my birth chart. I had read many books and learned the basics of astrology but had never delved past the surface.

The two-hour session totally captivated me. My chart showed what strengths I had gained in my past lives and the challenges or spiritual lessons I'd chosen to learn in this lifetime. I also learned that if a planet was presently orbiting the area of a birth planet, it triggered an event in my life. My session deeply intrigued me. I listened to the tape of the consultation many times over the next few months. I felt that this science was a true calling. I also learned that I was experiencing my first Saturn return, which happens at the age of twenty-nine and marks an important event or career opportunity.

I felt a strong desire to learn a lot more about this subject, so when Alexis suggested I join the American Federation of Astrologers, I took her advice. Alexis had visited their website often and told me that they provided home-study courses in astrology. I enrolled as a member and a student. I studied astrology every night after work. When I completed the curriculum and passed the final exam, I was a certified astrologer. In addition to learning the science, I'd naturally learned to interpret a chart intuitively.

I then provided astrology consultations in the evenings to coworkers and friends to build my confidence. After that I set up a website to advertise my business. I believed that I channeled higher wisdom and felt a natural high after I finished my sessions. I especially enjoyed assisting others. The practice gave me gratification.

In my spare time, my coworkers and I gathered to share dinner and drinks at different restaurants to expand our taste buds and get more familiar with our neighborhoods. One week, a coworker recommended a Thai restaurant located in a quaint shopping village called Old Hyde Park. She told me that her roommate's friend Steve was an employee there and that he was both gay and single. When I arrived at the restaurant, I had the feeling I'd been there before. As I stared at the front of the restaurant, I suddenly remembered the yellow awning from my initial relocation van tour of the city. *This is the restaurant I was drawn to in the small shopping village,* I remembered. *I wanted to eat here one day, and here I am.*

After dinner we all went to the bar, and my coworker introduced me to Steve. He was a handsome man with deep-blue eyes and a great smile. I sensed an instant mutual attraction. Steve provided free after-dinner cocktails to my coworkers and me, and we stayed around to chat. When his shift was over, Steve and I exchanged phone numbers. We went to dinner a week later and began dating around Christmastime.

Two months later on a rainy February afternoon, as I sat in my office doing last-minute work before catching a mid-afternoon business flight to the Midwest, I heard the phone ring. I hesitated to pick it up—I was running behind schedule and still had to finish packing my briefcase with my travel documents. I checked the caller ID just to be sure. The number looked vaguely familiar, but I couldn't place the caller. I answered it anyway.

"Hello?"

"Hi, Marty. It's Brock." His voice sounded shaky, like he was on the verge of tears.

"Hi. Are you okay?" I asked, clearing my chair and sitting down.

"I'm down here in Florida at my mom's house. My brother Luke died yesterday." Tears choked his words, and he broke into sobs.

I'd known that Luke had some physical ailments, including kidney disease, but I hadn't realized his condition was so severe. "What happened?" I asked, still numb from shock.

"He died of congestive heart failure."

I'd never known Luke had heart disease. My heart broke for him and for his family's loss. I contemplated canceling my business trip to attend the wake and funeral. I wanted to be there for Brock, but I was scheduled to attend a presentation at a major insurance group the next day. I was caught in a quagmire as I thought of the senior officials who were in flight from the New York office to meet me in Iowa that afternoon. The pressure was too great, so I told Brock I was heading to the airport on a business trip but that I was sorry for his loss and would call him as soon as I returned in two days. He said he understood and that he appreciated my condolences. I requested the funeral home information, and after hanging up, I ordered flowers to be sent to the wake.

I arrived at my hotel room with a heavy heart. I was only just starting to deal with the shock of Luke's death. I reminisced about our only encounter and felt heartbroken for Molly. I had a restless night's sleep thinking about Luke and his family. I prayed all night for them to heal from this sudden loss. I was also nursing a cold that had worsened on the flight. During the next two days, I medicated myself with cough medicine and aspirin to get through the trip.

Upon returning home, I immediately contacted Molly to express my sympathy. I then spoke with Brock and promised him I would call his mom regularly and visit her as often as I could over the next few months. He thanked me for my generosity and returned to New York.

Over the next couple of months, I developed a friendship with Molly. In our numerous phone conversations, we spoke often about death, grief, and healing. I had just read *Talking to Heaven* by James Van Praagh, which taught me more about life and physical death than any other book I'd ever read, and I recommended it to her. She read the book and found immediate comfort. She had already lost her parents and other relatives, but losing a child was enormously difficult for her. I promised her that the next time James Van Praagh taught a workshop or seminar anywhere in Florida, I would get tickets so we could attend. I wanted Molly to see James communicate with the afterlife. I wanted to give her an opportunity to see his work so she could believe that spirits survived physical death. More importantly, I hoped Luke's spirit would come through with a message.

Soon after my birthday, I traveled to east Florida to visit Molly. She seemed to be holding up well. I could see from her eyes that she was determined to heal.

Within minutes of my arrival, she grabbed my hand and sat me down. She seemed eager to talk, and she looked into my eyes as she spoke.

"I want to thank you from the bottom on my heart for telling Brock that you were gay," she began. "Brock contacted me the day after you told him because he was shocked. He had no idea you were gay. Brock had a fearful attitude toward gay people, and he was distant from his brother for years. Brock liked you very much, and once he realized you were okay and very normal, he realized his fears were unwarranted."

I stared wide-eyed. "Wow, I never knew that."

"After your admission, he got closer to Luke, and they had a full year of friendship before Luke's sudden death. I attribute that to your honesty and courage. It would be ten times more difficult to deal with Luke's death knowing that Brock hadn't been talking to him. The guilt alone would have killed Brock and me. Words cannot describe how grateful I am to you that they healed their relationship. I thank you immensely." She gripped my hand for emphasis.

I sat stunned. In coming out to Brock, I had intended to liberate myself, but it had liberated him. *Miracles do happen without our conscious control*, I thought. My intent that day was to lend my heart to a grieving mother, and in turn she elevated my spirits with her testimony. I spent the night and kept in touch.

When we worked in New York, my friend Evelyn and I had shared many discussions on spiritual topics. One summer, when she visited with family members in Tampa, Florida, she made time to visit me. We decided to spend a day together and scheduled a Sunday trip to Cassadaga, Florida, a small spiritualist camp known for its many psychics and mediums.

We attended the spiritual service at the local nondenominational temple. I enjoyed the service's format, which was different from the Catholic services I'd been raised in. The congregation was filled with mediums, who spoke of the connection between God and us. A tall, slender blonde woman with a beautiful voice sang "Let There Be Peace on Earth." After the service, Evelyn and I attended the free message session provided by student mediums at the town hall one block from the temple.

As we ate the cookies and drank the beverages provided, a student medium approached Evelyn and conveyed a message from her great aunt, saying that Evelyn would be moving soon. Evelyn looked surprised because on the drive, we had just discussed the possibility of her moving to Florida. After the student session ended, we ate lunch across the street at the landmark Cassadaga Hotel. Evelyn was happy she'd heard from her great aunt, who had raised her, but she longed to hear from her mother, who had died more than thirty years before. After lunch, Evelyn made an appointment for a reading with one of the six official psychics at the hotel. While I waited for her, I wandered around the holistic bookstore. When Evelyn exited the private session, she looked inspired and excited.

During our two-hour voyage home, we listened to the recording of Evelyn's reading. There was a background buzzing on the tape, which Evelyn said was from the window air-conditioning unit in the psychic's reading room. But toward the middle of the recording, the noise faded away to a dead silence. Then, to our disbelief, the psychic's voice faded as well, and another soft female voice said, "Regret is a useless feeling. Have no regrets." Then the buzzing sound came back and the psychic's voice returned.

I looked at the cassette player and then at Evelyn. I wondered if she had heard the same thing. I could tell by the wide-eyed look on her face that she had. I shut the tape off and we said simultaneously, "Did you hear that?" We could not believe what had happened. I rewound the tape a little and we listened again. Once again, the background noise diminished completely and the soft female voice repeated the same message. Chills ran up and down my spine the second time I heard it. I knew it was the voice of a deceased spirit.

Evelyn said, "I feel this is the voice of my deceased mother."

"You said you wanted to hear from her after your great aunt came through," I replied. "I guess she heard your request loud and clear. What a huge message."

Evelyn had recently contemplated leaving her job of twenty years to move to Florida, but she hadn't been sure if it was a good idea or something she might regret. Her mother's testimony gave her the courage to take the leap. We listened to the rest of the tape and then replayed the special message over and over until we arrived home.

For extra income, I took a part-time job as a fragrance model for the holidays and special events. During one promotional event, while walking alone through a department store, I had a mental flash of my life in the future. I was no longer in a relationship with Steve and no longer working for the bank. I had a position of responsibility and prominence, but the occupation was unclear. My inner voice said, "I will be going through major changes in two years." I didn't know how to react to this but felt that something significant was going to happen.

CHAPTER FIVE

REUNION

One evening Mother called me to say that after twenty-two years of estrangement, she wanted to reunite with her family. She asked me if I thought it was a good idea. I supported her quest and encouraged her to do so. In subsequent weeks, her initial research uncovered that her parents had passed away; that her lone sister, my aunt Nancy, had remarried; and that her older brother Jerry still lived in the same house. Mother decided she would approach Jerry first by paying him a surprise visit. I prayed for her courage and waited to hear how her visit had gone.

Mother called the first evening of her visit. She'd been very nervous but had just opened the front gate, walked up the stairs, and knocked on Jerry's door. This was the first time she'd set foot there in twenty-two years. When Uncle Jerry opened the door, he did not recognize Mother—but after she reintroduced herself as his sister, he hugged her and welcomed her visit. He gave her all the family updates: although her parents had died, all five of her siblings were still alive. Within days, Alexis met with Nancy, Jerry, and Dean. I spoke with Dean and Aunt Nancy from Florida shortly thereafter.

Although I hadn't missed speaking to or seeing Mother's family, I started to feel curiously excited. Mother planned a big family reunion within a few months. Aunt Nancy seemed more excited than anyone to reunite. She could not wait until the official reunion, so she flew down from New Jersey to Florida and visited with me privately so we could have quality time prior to the reunion. Despite my excitement, I was still trepidatious about getting too close too soon. Unconsciously, I still harbored anger toward the whole bunch. However, I was open to the possibility of having relationships with them, especially after Aunt Nancy's visit.

When I met her at the airport, I barely recognized her. I had blocked her out in my mind for so long; I'd forgotten what she looked like. She had aged well, and her appearance started to resonate with me. After many hugs and kisses, I drove her to my apartment. We ordered dinner and conversed.

She was very receptive and open. Within the first couple of hours, I knew this experience would reap rewards. I decided to ask her about the past.

"Why were you warm to me when outside of your house but cold and distant when inside?" I asked, trying to temper my tone with compassion.

Looking sad and regretful, she said, "I'm so sorry for everything. There was such a misunderstanding, and the whole separation should have never happened. I am very sorry for how everything turned out. The adults disagreed, but the kids paid the price of the separation"

Mother had never been honest with me about my father and her lineage. I felt that Aunt Nancy could provide me information about my earliest childhood, my parents, and my lineage, so I continued my questioning. "How was my parents' relationship?"

"Your parents did fight a lot, especially after Alexis was born. They had an abusive marriage that ended shortly after your birth."

"Where were you when I was born?"

"Your uncle Jerry and I went to the hospital with your mother when she went into labor with you. It was early evening, and your father wasn't around. You were born through cesarean section shortly after midnight."

This was important to me because I had learned through astrology that no birth is timed incorrectly. When the planetary positions are aligned to fulfill a person's divine script, the delivery signs are initiated and birth is imminent. I knew that Alexis had been delivered through cesarean section, and back in the sixties. When a mother delivered a child through cesarean, the subsequent children were delivered that way as well. I had always wanted to know when my official due date was or when my C-section had been scheduled. Hungry for more details, I pressed on.

"How was my mother's prenatal care of me? Did she rest enough? Was she nervous, angry, or upset? Was her environment filled with fear, anger, or anxiety? Did she drink or smoke?

Aunt Nancy bravely kept up with my relentless questions. "Unfortunately your parents fought a lot when she was carrying you."

"That makes sense. I've felt that from the moment I was incarnated, I was in survival mode. I felt I could never relax and that my parents' tumultuous relationship while in utero affected me that way."

"Your mother never drank or smoked while pregnant," Aunt Nancy continued. "You and Alexis stayed with me for quite awhile during and after your parents' painful divorce. I felt like you were my children, until I gave birth to Dean."

We ended the beautiful evening with a warm hug and forgiving energy. Aunt Nancy's weekend visit was healing for both of us. I learned a great deal about my grandparents and other ancestors too.

The official family reunion took place on a Sunday. The mid-September temperature was mild, in the eighties. Alexis and her boyfriend, Jake, hosted the event in their large backyard in Middletown, New Jersey. I enjoyed seeing my aunt, cousin, and uncle. We ate barbequed food, swam in the pool, laughed, and took loads of photos. Everybody seemed excited about reuniting. The evening ended around 11:00, and we all promised to keep in touch. Alexis, Dean, and I made plans to spend the next day together.

I headed to bed around midnight. I stopped by the kitchen area to say good night to Mother and Alexis, who was sipping her tea and listening to Mother talk about the reunion. I said my prayers and fell fast asleep.

I woke up at 7:00 the following morning. Everyone was still asleep, so I made coffee and read a magazine quietly in the kitchen. Alexis had written a note asking me to wake her up at 8:00, so I knocked on her bedroom door at the designated time, and she welcomed me in. As I approached her, she looked up and said, "Something unbelievable happened last night."

By the look in her eyes and the tone of her voice, I knew it was either serious or mysterious.

"Meet me in the kitchen in five minutes, and I'll tell you what happened," she said.

I was both excited and perplexed. As I walked back to the kitchen, I passed by the living room, where Mother was fast asleep on the couch, looking very peaceful. Her face had a healthy glow to it, almost angelic. I continued to the kitchen and waited for Alexis to arrive.

Alexis came in ten minutes later and poured herself a cup of coffee. She sat down and said, "Our grandparents visited from the other side last night."

"What do you mean?" I asked.

"Grandmother and Grandfather used my body to speak with Mother."

"You mean trance mediumship?"

"I don't know what they call it, but their spirits entered my body last night."

"What happened?"

"I don't remember everything, but it started early yesterday. I barely ate all day. I was busy running around making sure the reunion went well. I really wasn't hungry. I drank a lot of water and felt really light. Last night I drank two cups of decaffeinated herbal tea and was listening to Mother. Then something started to happen. I felt my heart rate slow down."

"Oh my God! What happened next?"

"I just faded. I can't explain it. I felt that I became suspended or frozen in time."

"I've read that's exactly what happens when a spirit enters a body in trance mediumship."

Alexis leaned forward, her eyes shining with excitement. "I don't remember who came through me or what they said. I just knew that something or someone used my body. It's hard to explain—I just know that's what happened."

"You're explaining it perfectly. I totally understand. This is amazing!"

"I remember that they exited through my chest. That fact I am very sure of."

"They exited through your heart chakra."

"I felt my heart rate increase and my body come back to life. Mother was holding my hand and saying, 'Please, God, don't take my daughter,' over and over again. Then she prayed the Our Father."

"Do you remember when this took place?"

"It happened around two in the morning."

I'd only gone to bed just after midnight. I tried to remember if I'd heard anything in my sleep. "I can't believe that you were still up talking with mother. Do you know how long they used your body?"

"Mother said it was a few minutes."

"Wow! This is incredible. They came through the day of the reunion. This has to be fated. I need to ask Mother what they said. If they expended so much energy to use your body, they must have had an urgent message to convey."

"Mother told me they spoke to her in Spanish." Like me, Alexis didn't speak or understand Spanish.

I looked forward to Mother awakening so I could get her side of this experience. Now I understood why she looked so angelic: she'd had an incredible encounter with the spirit world, and perhaps she'd been touched by an angel.

Alexis and I shared breakfast and then she went off to shower. At ten in the morning, I heard Mother wake up. When she entered the kitchen, I said, "Alexis briefed me on what happened last night. Please sit and tell me your side of the event."

"I was in the middle of a conversation with Alexis, but she wasn't responding to me. She looked stone-faced. I waved my hand in front of her face, but she didn't blink. I called her name over and over again. Then her face started to change, my heart started pounding, and my deceased mother's face appeared.

"My mother's voice came out of Alexis's mouth, speaking Spanish. She called me by the pet name I had when I was a child."

"This is incredible. What happened next?"

"She said, 'Please forgive me. I love you. Sorry I misunderstood you.'"

"What did you say?"

"I was in shock. I couldn't believe I was talking to my dead mother. She then said, 'Please help my son.'"

"Your brother?"

"Yes. I asked her which of my three brothers she meant. She said, 'You will know.'"

"This is amazing!"

"I panicked. I thought that Alexis was going to die. I wanted her back in her body. I told my mother to bring back my daughter, now!"

"What happened next?"

"Alexis's face changed again. This time my dead father's face appeared. He said in Spanish, 'I am protecting Alexis. Nothing will happen to her.' I didn't know what to believe, so I stood up, walked over to Alexis, and prayed that she wouldn't die. I asked God to bring her spirit back into her body. Slowly, she returned, and I was relieved."

This incredible story captivated me. I glanced to my right at a calendar hanging on the wall and noticed that the day before, the day of the reunion, was also Grandparents' Day. That was not a coincidence. I had learned from Aunt Nancy that Grandmother had died a lonely death. At the time of her passing, she was in touch with only two of her five children. She carried a heavy load to the other side. I hoped that my grandparents' visit would help Mother heal from her painful past. I then showered and prepared for my day with Alexis and Dean.

We met at a restaurant. This was the first time in our adult lives that we were all together. We had never discussed our parents' arguments and thought it would be advantageous if we talked about the subject so we could start off on the right foot. I wanted to clear the past so we wouldn't repeat the patterns in the future. Alexis videotaped us and created a documentary of that day.

Dean shared that he'd seen my mother when she visited her family a couple of weeks after the big disagreement back in the mid-seventies. She pleaded with her mother to speak with her, but Grandmother, who was stubborn and had a lot of pride, turned her back and ignored Mother, never to speak with her again. I now understood why Grandmother had come through Alexis to apologize and further understood my mother's anguish. Those of us gathered all agreed that we were not responsible for their disagreement.

After lunch, the three of us went on a journey to our old neighborhood, where Mother lived near Grandmother. There was graffiti on the front of the apartment building I'd lived in, and everything surrounding the building seemed much smaller. Then we visited our old Catholic school. While standing in front, Alexis noticed that one of the entrance doors was ajar, so she boldly entered and filmed the hallway. A woman appeared, walked toward us, and said, "Hello. I'm the vice principal. Can I help you?"

Alexis jumped in. "Hi. We graduated from this school in the 1980s, and we're filming a documentary of our lives. Can we enter the school to film our old classrooms?"

"Yes, you may. Please, come in."

I was shocked that the vice principal didn't ask for our identification or our names.

Alexis filmed the gym, cafeteria, and our classrooms. All three of us curious to see what had happened to our teachers, so before leaving, we stopped by the vice principal's office to thank her and ask some questions. She filled us in on who had died and who had retired.

I thought of the large substitute-teacher nun who had tried to choke me to death, so I asked, "Whatever happened to Sister Joan?"

"Sister Joan left the convent a long time ago. She is now married."

After a nice dinner together, the three of us ended our beautiful day, at peace with our new bond. I flew home the next day and spent some time digesting the whole reunion experience.

Mother's courage to reunite and heal from the past unconsciously influenced me, and so did Evelyn's deceased mom who said, "have no regrets" which stayed on my mind for a while. I'd also heard many successful people say, "Be courageous; you'll regret the things you didn't do more than the ones you did." This prompted me to take a risk and search for my father. I'd wondered for years if I'd ever see him again, and the uncertainty kept me in the past. It had been twenty-two years since I'd seen him.

I called Alexis the following day and relayed my intent. She agreed to assist me in my mission. All we knew about our father were his birth date and full name. We didn't know if he was dead or alive. Alexis agreed to pay for a search service on the Internet to gather his contact information, and I agreed to initiate correspondence and follow up on all leads. Her research showed that Father had been alive at least two years before and living in Texas. I suddenly remembered that Pearl, the now deceased psychic, had told me a decade earlier that he lived in Texas.

I sent a letter with my contact information to that address in Texas and awaited a response.

A week later I received a call.

"Hello?" I answered.

"Hi. Is this Martin?"

"Yes. Who's calling?"

"My name is Myra, and I believe we're cousins. I received a letter you're your address. Are you looking for your father?"

"Yes. Do you know him?"

"He's my uncle. My father is his brother. He lived with us until last year. He then decided to retire to Puerto Rico. Do you have a sister named Alexis?"

"Yes, I do."

"He always talked about you and Alexis. You two are his only children. I am so excited to speak with you! I have to admit, when I saw your letter, I thought it was a joke from my uncle, your father, because the handwriting is identical."

"Really? We have the same handwriting?" I asked, excited about the similarity.

"Yes, you do. I'm going to forward your letter to him and ask his permission to give you his address. I'll call you back when I contact him."

"Thanks! Please keep in touch. I look forward to hearing from you."

I hung up and thanked God for the link to my father. *What does he look like?* I wondered. *What does he do?* I had so many questions to ask him. I was so glad he was alive.

A week later Myra graciously called back and provided Father's address. "He doesn't have a phone, but you can reach him in writing," she said.

By Christmas, nearly three months had passed since my letter had been forwarded to Father, but still I had no response. I wondered if he'd received it. I decided to send him a Christmas card just in case.

Another month passed without reply. I was starting to feel that maybe I should detach from the situation. Then one afternoon, I was home from work during Martin Luther King Day, watching Oprah. The guest speaker was a male author who had written a book about estranged fathers and their children, and on the show, he counseled fathers who were about to reunite with their children. The reunions were emotional and cathartic. The author's main message to the estranged children was, "Please understand that fathers are just as scared and even more nervous to reunite than you. They have a lot of guilt. Please have patience, and don't give up easily."

That message was for me. It was a divine sign to persevere, have more patience, and hope. I gathered the strength to write a third and last time. I completed a light-hearted, forgiving, and loving letter.

On Valentine's Day 1999, I retrieved my mail and saw a letter with my father's return address. I stared at the handwriting and could not believe what I was holding. A feeling of bliss consumed me, and I hurried back into my apartment. I called Alexis, but she wasn't home, so I left a message on her voice mail telling her about the letter and asking her to call me as soon as she could.

I placed the unopened letter on top of my dining room table to wait until I heard from Alexis. I wanted to read it with her so we could share in the moment. Later that evening she finally called. I opened the letter and read it over the phone. I extracted an excerpt of the main massage and quoted it verbatim:

> Dear Son,
> How to start a communication after so many years with someone I haven't seen or heard is not easy. You are correct when you said we are almost strangers and yet being part of each other. Our separation was due to the worst enemy of marriage, divorce. (Mostly my fault!) Anyway, I did want to thank you for the Christmas card but I did not know what to say afterwards. I am so glad you wrote another letter. This time your words gave me something to where I could express a few things that may interest you. I hope my daughter and your mother are doing well. They were once "my little girls." I would like to embrace everyone and say, "Forgive me for what happened almost 30 years ago." Please give your mother my regards and I ask for forgiveness for all the inconveniences I caused. I was an immature Father and Husband. I hope my daughter writes to me.
>
> Love,
> Your Father

I reread the letter slowly so Alexis could type it verbatim on her home computer. Father sounded humble. I felt joy at the prospect of a new start, and I had a forgiving heart. I gave Alexis his address, and we each wrote him back. This time, I sent photos with my letter.

By this time, Steve and I had been dating for two years and living together. It was my first live-in relationship. We had settled in peacefully; but within a few months, the situation had become stressful. We had grown apart—we only existed.

Shortly after the big millennium New Year, I came across a prominent astrological website that offered many kinds of reports for sale. One report grabbed my attention—it profiled past lives and karmic obligations. I provided the birth data requested and ordered the report.

I was amazed at its accuracy. A lot of the information, including details about a past life filled with spiritual studies and healing abilities, rang true, but one paragraph in particular caught my attention: it stated that I carried an unconscious fear of abandonment and that it was most likely that my childhood would accentuate that fear.

That statement made perfect sense. I had always wondered why I unconsciously attracted men who were emotionally unavailable. I feared abandonment so deeply that I attracted men that would never leave me, yet once I had them to myself, I felt trapped and needed to escape.

The revelations continued. This fear was so ingrained in my subconscious that the universe in its perfect existence had continued to provide these conscious scenarios to me so that I could awaken to my self-destructive behavior.

The report provided other valuable advice, including that I listen to my dreams and incorporate behaviors such as meditation and yoga into my life. During a new moon in the zodiac sign of Aquarius, I purchased a journal and made a conscious effort to record my dreams. I said a prayer to the universe and asked for it to assist me in remembering my dreams. I learned so much from this online report.

I read many more books on metaphysical subjects and provided professional astrological consultations to clients and coworkers after work.

By now, my domestic environment had become unbearable. Each day, Steve and I grew more and more incongruous. I clearly saw that we had different philosophies on most things, including relationships, and within months, Steve moved out and we split up.

Within weeks, I had processed that making a commitment to live with Steve had triggered these unresolved issues within me. Since commitment is the opposite of abandonment, my making the commitment had been a good choice although the outcome had been unpleasant. But revelations about my relationships were not the only lessons that surfaced; the universe had many more amazing revelations and experiences up its sleeve.

CHAPTER SIX

TESTIMONY

I quickly acclimated to my peaceful surroundings. I meditated often and studied astrology every night. I had been checking James Van Praagh's website periodically to see when he would be lecturing in Florida, and to my enjoyment, he finally scheduled a visit in east Florida, south of Molly's house. I had promised to take her to see James, so I purchased the tickets online and told Molly about the event.

She elated but cautious. It had been two years since Luke had passed away, and she was still in pain from his loss. She said, "I don't want to get my hopes up too high." At the very least, I felt that it would help her better understand the life-after-death communication process.

When the tickets arrived at my house, I had a strong feeling something great was going to happen. I drove out the evening before and slept over at Molly's house. The morning of the event was exhilarating! I had the same great feeling come over me. I told Molly, "I feel that your parents will come through today."

She replied, "Oh my God, I forgot about them. I just want to hear from Luke."

Since I was headed back to the west coast of Florida after the event, we drove to the seminar in separate cars.

We arrived at spa and resort hotel's ballroom in Fort Lauderdale, Florida, five minutes before the event. The place was packed. We walked to the back and found two aisle seats on the right side. The stage was decorated with an elegant black backdrop and fresh flowers theatrically positioned in two huge vases on either side. Meditative music was being piped through the room, and the energy felt great.

James entered to thundering applause. He opened the session with a prayer and a quick synopsis of his background. He then led us through a meditation and some energy exercises. During the mediation, I felt that I left this earthly time zone and traveled into the wonderful eternal zone of another spiritual dimension.

After the meditation, James instructed those who were seated in odd-numbered rows to position their chairs to face the person behind them. A young, petite girl in her early twenties turned her chair around to face me. We greeted each other with a handshake and smiled in anticipation. Our first experience was an exercise in psychometry: identifying the mental impressions we received from a personal object such as a watch, ring, or bracelet from our partners.

My partner's name was Colleen. She handed me her bracelet, and I gave her my wristwatch. We closed our eyes for a few minutes, allowed the mental impressions to surface, and then opened our eyes to share our visions. I picked up only one impression from Colleen's bracelet: the word *friendship*.

When I told Colleen the word, she smiled with delight and said, "This was my best friend's bracelet. She passed away exactly a year ago today."

I replied, "I'm glad your best friend is around. This is a sign that she's alive and well in spirit."

Colleen picked up only one impression from my watch: a vision of the pyramids in Egypt. It didn't ring any bells with me at first. It was only later that I learned about my Egyptian past, including the lifetime in which I served as an astrology scribe.

In the next exercise, we were instructed to look directly at our partner's faces and examine the area surrounding the head and shoulders to see the other's aura. Then the lights were turned off, leaving the room totally dark. My eyes quickly acclimated to the darkness, and I saw Colleen's face. What happened next completely astonished me. Her face went completely black, and I just saw the outline of her long, dark hair. Next, a skeletal face appeared. Chills ran through my body. I sat very still to make sure what I had just witnessed had actually been real. Again, Colleen's face went black, and the skeletal face reappeared. I sat memorized by it for the next few minutes, until the lights were turned back on.

James encouraged us to share what we had seen without filtering the information. This time Colleen went first. She said, "I saw your aura. There were many bright colors that vibrated around your shoulders, and you had a white halo over your head."

I was surprised and relieved that she had seen only my aura. But now it was my turn. As carefully as I could, I said, "Your face changed often. It went completely black, and then a frail and skeletal face appeared. The face was withdrawn, sunken, and had angular bone structure."

Colleen stared at me without a word. Uncomfortable now, I shrugged, only half believing what I'd just witnessed.

For the next half hour, many of the audience members shared their experiences with the crowd. I heard incredible testimonies and visions. We were then instructed to return our chairs to their initial positions. At that point, Colleen leaned toward me and said, "I almost died a few months ago. I was a skeleton suffering from anorexia."

I gasped and fell back into my chair. I finally understood my vision. I said, "Please take care of yourself; your life is so very meaningful."

She replied, "I agree. That's why I'm alive today."

After a lunch break, the seminar resumed. The afternoon session provided more psychic development techniques, which we practiced on other audience members. In one such exercise, we were instructed to scan the person in front of us with our hands to detect any physical ailments. We shared our experiences with our partners, and then James encouraged audience members to share their experiences with everyone.

Molly raised her hand, and James found her like he was using radar and picked her. He summoned an assistant to give her a hand-held microphone. While Molly stood waiting for the microphone, James said, "You are a healer. I see white light all around you."

James then proceeded to bring through messages from both Molly's parents and her son, Luke. After the event, Molly was mobbed by well-wishers. I spoke with her briefly, feeling her joy and amazement. She confirmed everything James had said. I hugged her good-bye and drove back home, thinking about the day's event. I was amazed that Molly was one of only ten chosen from the crowd of more than one thousand people—all of whom had attended in hopes of receiving messages through James. This experience validated my earlier feeling that something great was going to happen today. I had tapped in to the fact that Molly's parents would come through—I knew this would happen before it became manifest in the physical world. Since this experience seemed to be preordained, I knew I needed to seek further spiritual truths.

As I prepared for bed one evening, I noticed Cashmere walking in and out of her litter box. I watched her do this for five minutes and noticed she released a small amount of urine each time. Intuitively, I felt she had contracted another bladder infection—a complication from diabetes, a diagnosis she'd received a few months prior. But it was two in the morning, I had no medication to give her, and I was very tired. Instead of driving her to a twenty-four-hour animal hospital, I felt guided to apply hands-on healing.

I laid her on her side and placed my right hand over her bladder area. I closed my eyes and prayed, "God, please send the white light of the Christ Consciousness to radiate through my hand and heal her bladder." I repeated this prayer for two minutes until Cashmere turned over and walked away. I sat on the floor and observed her for a few minutes. Rather than go into the litter box, she curled up in bed and fell fast asleep. The following morning, I saw her use the litter box and heard indications of a healthy bladder. I thanked God for the miracle of healing my cat. This was the first time I'd used hands-on healing, and it had worked!

In my attempt to heal from my past, especially my twenty-two-year estrangement from my father, he and I had written each other three times and exchanged pictures as well. It was my turn to write him again, and this time I struggled to find the words. At this point I felt a need to initiate a deeper connection with him. We had neither spoken on the phone nor visited each other in the entire year since we'd reconnected, all by his choice. He only felt comfortable and safe in writing. I felt frustrated.

I longed to heal my absent father's pain. I really wanted to look him in the eyes and tell him I loved him, and I wanted to hug him so badly, but I would have gladly accepted a phone relationship so I could at least hear his voice again. I had forgotten what he sounded like.

I didn't know what else to share besides the usual surface conversation. I had written about my desires, education, and feelings. In an attempt to take the relationship to another level, I wrote a loving letter expressing my desire to either meet him in person in any location or to speak with him on the phone. I supplied him my home and work numbers again. I mailed the letter and hoped for the best. He never responded.

I had been injecting Cashmere with insulin twice a day, but I woke up one Saturday morning to her having a seizure. The vet had warned this might happen, so I kept a bottle of syrup handy just in case her sugar levels dropped. As she trembled and cried uncontrollably, I immediately spattered syrup in her mouth. She calmed down within seconds. I rushed her to the animal hospital, and the vets admitted her overnight to regulate her sugar. The blood work showed that all her organs were functioning well. I picked her up the next day, held her in my arms like a baby, looked into her beautiful Siamese blue eyes, and said, "Please let me know when you want to go to the spirit world. Please give me a clear sign when you are ready, and I will honor it. As long as your organs are functioning, I will not put you to sleep." After her stay in the hospital, she bounced back.

But a month later she fell ill again. This time she vomited uncontrollably. I took her to the animal hospital again, and the vets gave her a shot to stop her vomiting. Tests of her sugar levels were so high that they surpassed the reading marker. She was kept overnight again to stabilize her condition. I picked her up the next day and was instructed to follow up with her regular vet. I took her home and closely monitored her behavior. She didn't eat or drink or use the litter box the entire day. She just slept or lay there looking around. My mother happened to be visiting, so I asked her to monitor Cashmere while I went to work the following day.

That afternoon, Mother called crying while I was at work. She told me that for the last few hours, Cashmere had been sitting on a chair looking disoriented and weak. She hadn't had a drop of food or water in almost thirty-six hours. I knew this was the end, that it was time to put her to sleep. The realization gave me a lump in my throat. I spoke with my manager, who was a cat lover as well, and she let me leave work early. I drove home in tears, thinking about the nearly eighteen years Cashmere had spent with me.

I entered my home and asked Mother if she would drive to the vet so I could hold Cashmere in my arms on the way. I didn't want to come back home with an empty animal carrier. When we arrived, the vet drew Cashmere's blood.

I then sat in the waiting area holding my cat, waiting for someone to come through and give me the results.

Suddenly my lethargic cat reached up to my face and nudged my earlobe with her nose. *Oh my God! I have just received the sign I asked for last month. She just said good-bye.*

Minutes later we were summoned into a private room. The veterinarian walked in and said, "Cashmere has kidney failure. Her kidneys have stopped functioning. It would best to put her to sleep." I cried because I had known it was time.

The vet stepped out to give my mother and me as much time as we needed to say good-bye. After a few minutes, I summoned the doctor. With tears spilling from my eyes and a heavy heart, I held Cashmere's precious face, looked into her blue eyes, and whispered, "Go to the light." With that, she peacefully left her body.

Cashmere's death was not only a painful loss but also the end of my long unconscious life. I was not prepared for what awaited me, but it came anyway.

CHAPTER SEVEN

PLUTO

Still grieving from the loss of Cashmere and simultaneously enlightened by the profound dream of her that told me to see myself as a student of everything and a victim of nothing, that the earth is only a schoolroom in which we learn to love.

It had now been two years since I had walked through a department store and experienced a flash and heard my inner voice say that my life would go through major changes.

One evening, after I parked my car in the space designated for my condo, I saw home repairmen painting the vacant condo below the one I lived in. The residents had suddenly moved out, and the place was being repainted. As I walked up the stairs to my rented condo, one of the repairmen, a well-mannered gentleman in his forties, stepped out to greet me.

"Excuse, me, are you interested in buying a condo?" he asked.

"No," I answered politely, and I continued on to my home.

Three evenings later I saw the same repairman installing carpet, and I quickly ran up the stairs to avoid another exchange.

As I approached the top step, I heard him shout, "We're almost done fixing up your condo!"

I pretended not to have heard him, hurried into my place, and locked the door. I wasn't sure why I felt so uneasy, so I sat outside on my back deck to figure it out. I hadn't been thinking about moving and hadn't saved money to purchase property, yet every time I tried to dismiss the idea of buying, I felt a nagging uncertainty. I couldn't rationalize my feelings. *Is the universe pushing me to buy this home?* I thought about my rented condo and realized that my lease had expired two months before. Oddly, the usually efficient landlord had not sent the renewal notice yet, although I had reminded her twice. It occurred to me that if I wanted to buy property, I could borrow the down payment and closing costs from my 401(k). After thinking this through, I decided to meet the repairman the following day, tour the condo, and find out the price. As soon as I made this decision, a feeling of peace flowed through me, dispelling my uneasiness.

The following day I saw a neighbor who had just purchased a similar condo. I introduced myself, we briefly chatted about the neighborhood, and she voluntarily told me what she had paid for her condo. I thanked her and secretly wondered if the universe was paving the way for my possible negotiation. The price she had given was very affordable. I felt excited!

I prayed for courage, approached the owners later that day, and officially met Todd—the repairman and owner's son.

Todd gave me a tour of the condo. It had a large master bedroom with a walk-in closet, vanity area, full bath, and two large windows. The spare bedroom had two large closets and another full bath. The living and dining areas made up a large great room. There was also a linear kitchen with eighteen cabinets—enough to store my culinary appliances and gadgets—and an outdoor deck. The freshly painted white walls, the new tiles in the kitchen and bathrooms, and the new tan carpeting in the other rooms gave the place a pristine look. Because it was a corner condo, it had plenty of windows to bring in more natural sunlight.

"Well," Todd said. "Nice, isn't it?"

I agreed.

"So make me an offer. My mom owns the condo; she's in her eighties and just wants to get rid of it."

I offered three thousand dollars less than what my neighbor had paid.

"Well, that seems fair," Todd responded. "Let me think about it. What's your telephone number?"

We shook hands, and I felt like a boulder had lifted from my shoulders. A couple of days later Todd approached me and accepted my offer. I provided him additional contact information, and he mentioned that his brother-in-law, who worked for a title company, would contact me to sign a contract.

As an astrologer, I always tried to stay informed about current movements of the planets. However, as I went through the process of buying the new condo, I was working full-time at my corporate job and preparing for my relatives' ten-day Thanksgiving visit, so I didn't have time to keep up with the latest astrological shifts. I waited until after Christmas to resume following the celestial movements.

In the meantime, I settled into a daily routine at work. Thursday evening was always my bowling night. Besides reducing stress, the sport allowed me to spend fun time with my favorite coworkers. My bowling league was filled with mostly conservative, backward people. Aside from my friends, I was the only one with all my own teeth—and certainly the only gay person. But I managed to have fun anyway and overlook my opponents' dental shortcomings.

After one particular bowling session, my teammate Sue approached me and asked, "Can you talk to my friend Rick about his astrology chart? I met him last month and am very attracted to him, so I'm wondering if we're astrologically compatible. He only lives five minutes away." She told me his birth details.

"Rick has the same birth date as me," I replied, astonished. "In fact, he was born within a few hours of me in the same year, just a few miles away!"

"Oh!" Sue exclaimed. "I thought his birth date was similar to someone I knew but couldn't remember who."

Has Rick experienced similar life circumstances as me? I thought.

It was eleven in the evening, and I'd been looking forward to going home and getting a good night's rest. Although I usually didn't do things spontaneously, I felt a burst of energy and intuitively felt good about going with Sue to Rick's place.

We parked our cars and walked upstairs to Rick's apartment. As we approached the top, Sue asked, "After we leave, please tell me if you think Rick might be gay." Silently, I had wondered the same thing, since Rick and I shared similar charts. But I didn't say anything—I didn't want to insinuate that every person born on my birth date was divinely scripted to be gay.

We knocked and were welcomed in. I shook Rick's hand, looked him in the eye, and said hello. Rick was a moderately handsome guy around six foot three and muscular. He wasn't wearing a shirt, flaunting his well-built chest. I immediately sensed he was gay but kept it to myself.

I sat on a stool in the kitchen while Sue opened a bottle of merlot and poured three glasses. We toasted each other and sipped the wine. Rick then excused himself to use the bathroom. While Sue and I awaited his return, I glanced around his apartment and noticed books similar to ones I owned, especially dream texts, in his entertainment center. The room was decorated with lit candles, giving it a romantic and spiritual energy. Rick's beautiful black Persian cat, Chloe, walked toward me, stopped at the foot of my stool, rolled over on her back, and stared at me. I gazed into Chloe's eyes and saw the spirit of Cashmere looking back. I was momentarily taken aback.

Rick returned and said, "Oh my God! I am shocked to see Chloe out in front of company. She always hides in the bedroom when company visits."

Chloe then stood up and pranced into the bedroom. I told Rick and Sue about Cashmere's recent passing, Chloe's eyes, and the profound dream I had experienced three days after Cashmere's death. Although both of them were amazed, Rick seemed especially captivated by my dream and Chloe's unusual behavior.

After our glass of wine, we went into the computer room to run an astrological birth chart for Rick. He was excited and receptive to what I had to say. He confirmed the specifics I provided.

We finally ended the gathering with hugs and promises to get together for drinks around Christmastime. Sue and I said good night to Rick and left.

When we reached our cars, I told Sue that although I had initially thought Rick was gay, I wasn't too sure. She agreed with my opinion, and we both drove home. I put the matter out of my mind.

Two weeks later Sue called to tell me that Rick had admitted he was gay and in the middle of a breakup. She also said, "Rick enjoyed your company and feels he can trust you. He really needs support right now. He wanted me to give you his number so you can contact him."

That evening after exercising, showering, and eating dinner, I finally sat down to call Rick. I dialed his number, and the phone rang several times without answer. I was about to hang up and try again when I heard a hurried voice say, "Hello."

"Rick? It's Marty."

Rick blurted out, "I need to call you back!"

"Okay," I said, feeling brushed off. "Do you want my number?"

"No, I have it on the caller ID. Thanks for calling." And he hung up.

I felt immediately uncomfortable. I sensed some drama or deceit and didn't want any part of it. I resolved to listen and stay detached if he actually returned my call.

A couple of days later Rick finally called back. He apologized for hanging up so abruptly. He proceeded to tell me all about his breakup predicament. I listened and offered suggestions to minimize drama, and we ended the conversation with good vibes.

I closed escrow on my new condo right after Christmas and started packing for the move. I decided not to provide astrological consultations for a few weeks until I settled in my new home. Subsequently, I further delayed following the current celestial movements of planets, or the speed with which each planet orbits the sun, listed in a book called an *ephemeris*. I was also speaking to Rick more often. Despite my earlier resolve to stay detached, my feelings for him had deepened.

I moved three days before the end of the year 2000. I was glad to have family and friends to assist with the move and to celebrate the purchase. On New Year's Day, Alexis, Mother, and I took a four-hour midnight cruise from St. Petersburg Beach to ring in 2001. I invited Rick to join us. He accepted, and everyone had a good time.

A few days later I decided to take two weeks' vacation so I could unpack and chill out. My family and friends had left, and I needed to replenish my energy. My feelings for Rick were increasing daily. Our conversations were incredible—our thoughts and feelings seemed completely synchronized. We shared many parallel interests and experiences, and I felt he was my soul mate. However, I was fully aware that he had just ended a relationship, and I did not want to be his rebound. I also knew I wasn't emotionally ready to be intimate with someone. So I fought off my feelings and kept our relationship platonic.

A week into my vacation, I woke with a heavy feeling on my chest. I sat in the dining room to drink my coffee and started to cry. I cried on and off for half an hour, not understanding why. I felt my heart open up and flood with joy for my new home and for Rick. I went to the beach that day, as I had often done throughout my life, to reconnect and reenergize.

Another week passed. During our daily conversations, Rick spoke frequently about his recent ex-lover, and this made me realize that Rick wasn't over him yet. I kept my feelings guarded and my heart sheltered.

When I returned to work, I walked into a nightmare of piled-up work and corporate drama.

While I was excited to own and move into my new home, my stress level had increased, and I started losing weight. I felt nervous, anxious, stressed, and insecure. I also had fits of rage, which scared me. I struggled to control this atypical behavior.

Upon arriving home one evening, I ran a bath. I shut off my phones, lit a candle, turned off all the lights, sat in the tub, and focused on my breathing. I finally relaxed.

After a few minutes, I heard my inner voice say, "Get more sleep. You need to heal your emotions."

I heeded that advice by skipping dinner and heading straight to bed, and I slept soundly for ten hours.

The following week was an emotional roller coaster. I often broke down and cried over a sad song or memory while driving to work. I had anxiety attacks. The first time it happened, I felt a wave of pure panic crash over me. I freaked out! I had never experienced these feelings before, so I smoked more cigarettes and drank more alcohol to sedate myself. I thought my repressing my feelings for Rick might have triggered this change. I debated whether I should confront him about my feelings or detach from him completely.

Mother had come to stay with me one weekend and was alarmed by my behavior. With extreme concern, she said, "I've never seen you in so much pain." There were times I couldn't see anything, I felt so enraged!

One evening a wave of anger came over me, and I slammed doors and threw everything in sight. I was out of control. Just before slamming the kitchen cabinet shut, I heard my inner voice say, "Martin, how are you going to help other people heal if you can't heal yourself?"

Stunned by the declaration, I stopped and slowly closed the cabinet door. I sat and contemplated what that statement meant. What did I need to heal?

Like a script from a romance novel, one evening, Rick called and expressed deeper interest in dating. He included me in his plans, spoke less of his ex-lover, and insinuated a romantic connection.

Tampa hosted the Super Bowl January 2001. Rick came over to watch the game with me and spent the night. We started dating thereafter, and I hoped my anxiety would diminish for good.

The following week, Brock called to tell me that he planned to visit his mom in Florida the following week and that he wanted to catch a basketball game in Orlando. The New York Knicks were scheduled to play the Orlando Magic. I agreed to meet him there. I looked forward to sharing another basketball memory with Brock, as we had many times at Madison Square Garden.

The morning before I met Brock, I attended mass at the nondenominational temple. Afterward, I purchased lavender and sage incense and oil at a nearby metaphysical bookstore, where I met a woman named Carol, a sleek and chic sixty-year-old wearing a vibrant purple-and-gold dress. Carol photographed auras with a special camera. She had a loving presence about her. The sample display of images intrigued me, so I decided to have my own aura photographed. I sat down and placed my hands flat on some metal plates, and Carol draped me in a black cape. She instructed me to take a deep breath and look into the camera.

After she snapped my picture, Carol interpreted the colors in my photo.

"There is unhealed grief shading your heart chakra," she began.

She then shared a story about how she had healed from her painful relationship with her deceased mother, who had abandoned Carol during an emotional time in her life. She told me that she was tired of being angry, so she sat in a chair and placed another one in front of her. She envisioned her mom sitting in the empty chair, and she vented all her painful feelings to her imaginary mother. As Carol's tears flowed, she let go of the anger and healed her strained relationship with her mother.

"My mother's behavior taught me valuable lessons of independence," she concluded.

I thanked Carol for the insight. I looked forward to healing my heart chakra. In the meantime, I drove to join Brock for dinner and the basketball game.

Brock and I had a wonderful dinner. We reminisced about the years we'd spent following the Knicks together. After dinner we walked through downtown Orlando and then headed for the game. The Knicks lost that night, but we had a good time anyway. Brock planned to sleep over at my place so he could see my new condo, but local brush fires were blocking the main Interstate, so we were stuck in traffic until the wee hours and had to sleep in a hotel instead. The following day, Brock had to head back to his mother's, but he promised to stop by and see my condo the next time he visited Florida.

I drove home with the same heavy feelings in my chest. I remembered what Carol had said regarding my unhealed grief. I needed to cry to release the heaviness. When I thought about whom I had not grieved for yet, Father came to mind. He wasn't physically gone, but he seemed dead in my life. He hadn't replied to my last letter, and our relationship was still in limbo.

I sat in my home office and put an empty chair in front of me. I took a deep breath and envisioned my father, and the tears streamed out of my eyes. I envisioned myself as the eight-year-old boy looking into the mirror with a broken heart. I told my imaginary father, "I only wanted to feel loved!" Those were the only words I could muster. I cried my eyes out. Once the tears had passed, I knew I could move on.

But the relief from dating Rick and grieving for my father was short-lived. My anger and anxiety came back and persisted throughout my workweek. I determined to relax the entire weekend. On Saturday, after a late-afternoon nap, I woke up feeling dazed and light-headed, with a constant pressure in my head. I felt something was happening to me beyond my control—a strong invisible force giving me a sense of doom. I needed to get fresh air, so I went to the local state fair.

I wandered around the fair for three hours, feeling as if my feet didn't touch the ground. I looked at the adults and children enjoying the rides and playing the games. I couldn't feel their enjoyment. I felt completely out of my body. Even after eating dinner and drinking water, I still felt dazed. I stopped at a booth to play a game and won a huge glass punch bowl. After winning, I decided to head back home but was so disoriented that I couldn't find an exit. I wandered around aimlessly, lost. My arms felt like they might fall off from carrying the heavy punch bowl. I finally asked someone to assist me, and he guided me out to the parking lot.

When I arrived at my car, I placed the punch bowl on the front passenger seat, sat behind the wheel, and relaxed for a moment. I then received a clairvoyant vision of a page from my astrology forecast report showing current celestial trends affecting the birth chart. The page contained the title of an astrological transit: "Pluto Square Natal Moon." Below this, the text said, "Deep psychological change will take place. Waves of anger, panic, and anxiety are common. Childhood issues, domestic changes, and parent relationships will be affected."

Stunned by the clarity of my vision, I suddenly remembered that I hadn't been following my astrological forecast report, which would have reminded me about the current planetary movements and their impact on my specific birth chart. I had forgotten the old adage that "to be forewarned is to be forearmed."

I drove home to look for my forecast report. I knew it was still packed away from my move, but I was determined to find it that night. Upon arrival, I picked through boxes until I located it. Reading through it, I was amazed to discover what had been happening. My life was going through a major two-year transformation. The report revealed why I felt emotionally fragile—the condo purchase, my relationship with my parents, and my deep-thought state of mind.

I then realized that anxiety, frustration, and anger are exacerbated by the resistance to heal. This was a *huge* revelation for me. Now I didn't have to feel like I was having a nervous breakdown, unless I continued resisting. I was relieved to know where these forces emanated from, and why. Things started to look clearer, but this initial upheaval was only the beginning. What took place in the next couple of years completely transformed my life.

The next morning I woke to a leak in my bathroom. I called in late to work and contacted a plumber. I continued with my morning ritual—entering a prayer on an Internet prayer circle and meditation. While waiting for the plumber, I sat and listened to a mellow CD.

Suddenly I felt an upward shift in my chest and a burst of emotion come forth. I started to cry, and the tears kept coming. This time, I leaned on the pain, embraced it, and allowed it all to surface. I cried for twenty minutes and went through many tissues. I grieved for everything from my past. I finally stopped crying so I wouldn't scare the plumber when he arrived. After that emotional cleansing, I felt light as a feather, naturally high, and healthy. I determined to further pursue my astrology interests and take better care of myself.

My dream state was very active during this emotional upheaval, and I had many dreams that involved water. After my strong emotional release, my dreams became more stable. I realized that water symbolized emotions, and it was a wonderful gauge for my emotional healing.

Then one evening I had the following dream of my deceased grandmother:

I shopped for fruit, vegetables, and spices at a farmer's market. My grandmother was standing behind the spice counter. When I approached, she handed me the spices I wanted to purchase. She knew exactly what I needed and gave them all to me. I said, "*Gracias*," which means "thank you" in Spanish, she prepared to say, "*De nada*"—"you're welcome"—but I chimed in and said it for her. She looked at me and started laughing. She thought what I had done was very kind. Not only had I spoken for her, but I also spoken in Spanish. When she first handed me the spices, her eyes had looked pensive and vulnerable, but after the verbal exchange, her eyes were filled with warmth and love. We both felt an understanding and acceptance. It was a joyous experience. In the background, I saw Aunt Nancy watching this exchange and smiling at both of us.

When I woke up, I felt surprised. I had neither seen nor dreamt about my grandmother since the family estrangement when I was eight, and my relationship with her before that had been distant and detached. She was not an affectionate person, and I sensed that she was bitter.

Another huge barrier was that she only spoke Spanish and I only spoke English.

After learning about my grandmother's life from Aunt Nancy, I had a more compassionate understanding of her. She'd had a rough life; losing her mother when young, burying a four-year-old son, and enduring a husband's infidelity. I understood her pain and subsequent behavior. I believed it was my new mind-set that allowed my grandmother to come through. Her visit touched me, and I felt that our relationship had mended.

The realization that a force greater than me was working behind the scenes helped me to resist panic and anxiety. In fact, I was learning to embrace these feelings, and I no longer feared them. This was a blessed choice on my part because the anxiety started to diminish substantially. To further reduce my anxiety, I engulfed myself in reading material to learn more about the Pluto transit. I went to bookstores or libraries during my lunch hour to read the perspectives of other astrologers. I wanted to do my part to mitigate the intensity of this transit.

Meanwhile, my emotional attachment to Rick was continuing to intensify. Our psychic connection was incredible—as if we were meant to be together. However, I noticed inconsistencies with some of his stories. He would tell me about his day at work, and then I would find out through the grape vine that he had actually had that day off. This only heightened my insecurity.

I read Marianne Williamson's *A Return to Love* for some relationship advice. The book's messages and my personal experiences conflicted, especially about forgiveness. I had always thought that forgiveness was accepting the painful things that had happened to you, but I later learned that I didn't have to condone painful things; I just had to learn from them and let them go. I strongly felt that Rick was my soul mate, but his behavior often made me question my assumption. I initially thought the book's information hindered my intent, but learning its truths would later liberate me for good.

As time went on, Rick distanced himself from me. He often cancelled plans at the last minute, avoided my phone calls, and didn't call back as promised. Rick's distance only created more pain for me in my mentally depleted state. He always had an excuse. I asked myself why I was trying to be Marty the Martyr. I would never have tolerated such behavior from anybody else, yet had never felt so strongly for another. I loved and hated him at the same time. After he cancelled plans again, I finally advised him that I needed some space.

I was at a breaking point and needed to make a decision. That evening, I prayed for a dream to provide clear signs about my relationship. I specified that if I remembered any of my dreams and received a clear message, I would forgive and stay with Rick. If I didn't, I would walk away for good. I awoke with no recollection of any dreams, so I deduced it was a sign to walk away from the relationship.

In the Internet prayer circle created by Deepak Chopra I contributed to, I entered a message indicating that I was grateful to have received an answer to my dream request. I understood that no was my answer, and I looked forward to ending this painful relationship with Rick. I hit the Send button to post my prayer.

I received a pop-up window indicating that my prayer couldn't be posted. I thought that was strange—I had never encountered such a message, and I'd posted hundreds of prayers before. I logged out and logged back in, retyped the same prayer, and hit Send, and I received the same rejection. Bewildered, I sat back and contemplated what was going on. I was then impressed with the following statement:

The prayer typed is not correct.

I reread the initial prayer and realized I had written it out of anger instead of love, so I decided to change it. I also felt that perhaps ending the relationship was not the answer. I reworded the prayer with a loving message. I hit the Send button, and the new prayer posted instantaneously. This experience mystified me all day long. To get me through that day, I drove to a park after work and swung on the adult swing for over an hour, trying to reach the sun, subconsciously hoping it would rescue me from my turmoil. I found the tallest and thickest oak tree and hugged it until it hurt. I needed comfort.

The following week, I felt restless, in desperate need of guidance regarding Rick and my life's direction. Part of me wanted to hold on to him, while the other part wanted to let him go. I hadn't seen any clear messages about which path I needed to take. My astrology forecast report didn't mention anything about intimate unions. I decided to see a psychic medium named Mike, whom I had heard on a local radio show one morning. I found his number in one of the town's holistic healing magazines and made an appointment for the following week.

It was a Tuesday evening. I drove to the appointment after work. I entered Mike's housing complex and noticed that the numerical password to enter the gated community added up to 11. I also realized that his apartment number added up to 11 as well. Intuitively, I felt his life-path number had to be 11. In numerology, 11 is a master number; it represents the humanitarian and the spiritual leader. I felt comfortable with this knowledge and parked the car. I said a prayer asking that Mike be used as an instrument to provide me with the spiritual direction I sought. I walked up to his home and rang the bell.

A man in his sixties answered the door wearing a colorful *corda*, an Indian garment used for prayer. I immediately felt his energy was authentic. He introduced himself, shook my hand, and invited me in. He guided me to his plush living-room couch and sat on a cushioned chair across from me.

"You have a super sensitive aura," he said in a soothing voice. "It is an aura that many healing practitioners have. You are a natural counselor. Do you have one question you seek an answer to?"

"I need to know if I should stay in or leave my present relationship," I responded.

"Please supply me with your and your partner's birth dates," Mike requested.

"It's the same for both of us," I replied and gave him the birth date.

"You are very intuitive," Mike said. "You possess a great third eye. You have a great memory and a strong subconscious mind. You travel astrally, communicate with spirits, and have incredible dreams.

You are in a major transitional period in your life—it is a strong period of change that will last a couple of years and bear fruit for the rest of your incarnation.

"I see you writing many books, being an entrepreneur, and speaking to groups of people. You will develop an identity, a personality, that will bring you personal gratification. You will travel and be very successful, but you must plan your work and work your plan."

Mike proceeded to communicate with spirits I had shared past lives with. These spirits were guides assisting me on my earthly mission.

"You have a male spirit you shared a lifetime with in Egypt," he continued. "He said that you were a scribe in astrology during that lifetime."

I was shocked since Mike didn't know I was an astrologer.

He continued, "You were also a Mexican Indian from the Mayan ruins and had another lifetime as a priest or a monk in Italy."

The priest or monk lifetime rang true to me.

He told me to put physical intimate relationships on the back burner for the moment because I was going through a spiritual preparation. He indicated that during the evolutionary phase, I would have difficulty relating to others. However, he told me to connect with visionaries and conscious spiritual beings.

"The next two years will bring great illumination that will move you to a higher vibration," Mike continued. "You will work with the top three chakras: the crown, clairvoyant, and throat. All this will heighten your mental capacity for alchemy."

He further enlightened me by saying, "This current force that you are experiencing is pure divine will. Answers to your life come through meditation and prayer. Please read Psalm 23 in the Bible"

He ended the incredible session by declaring, "You lived as an Essene, in the time before Jesus."

I drove home feeling relaxed and amazed. In my condo, I reread the notes I had written during the session and sat still to allow the experience to sink in. I felt that I had received a clear answer to my question about Rick. I tried to make sense of why this relationship had surfaced at all. I had been through breakups before, had shed the tears, learned the lessons, and moved on. However, here I stood at thirty-two years of age, unable to shake Rick from my being. I wondered why I had trouble letting him go. A month had passed in which I hadn't spoken with Rick at all, but I still felt wounded. I got through one day at a time.

It was now springtime, and I took a weekend trip to visit Eli, who had relocated from New Jersey to Arizona. I accompanied him to Sunday church service. The pastor read a passage from the Bible and started her sermon. Suddenly I saw a beautiful white light emanating from her head. I stared at her for a moment, turned away briefly to clear my vision, and then faced her again. The light was still surrounding her from shoulder to shoulder, about a foot wide all around. I looked around the altar to check for a reflection from the church lights, but I didn't find any.

I shifted in my seat a few times to see if anything changed with a different angle. But the aura was brighter than ever. I accepted that this was not my imagination, and I marveled at it. This was the first time I'd seen an aura. After the mass, Eli asked if I had been okay during the service. He had noticed that I'd been a bit restless. I told him what I had seen, and he was amazed. After the mass, I greeted the pastor and shared my vision with her. She gracefully accepted my revelation and said simply, "God is good." I flew back to Tampa feeling better.

When I arrived home one evening after work, I opened my door to enter my condo and was hit with a strong familiar scent. I stopped and realized it was the scent of my deceased cat, Cashmere. I acknowledged her spiritual presence and felt my mood elevate. I was astonished by the strength of her scent. I had forgotten what she smelled like because she had died before I'd moved. Her presence felt loving and supportive. I viewed it as a sign that my life was mending.

I had always had a fascination with life after death, and I had satisfied my curiosity by reading books and attending seminars in which mediums communicated with the afterlife. I continued healing by reading loads of spiritual texts. I also started documenting quotes, thoughts, and prophetic statements that spontaneously came to mind. This inspiration increased daily, and I noticed that these thoughts were spiritual. The messages helped me stay focused. I received secrets or truths about the universe.

One particular truth was revealed to me: the purpose of time is for you to awaken to the spirit within—and to enjoy that awakening on earth. Your enjoyment will illuminate others, therefore awakening them, and it will spread further. Time exists to measure linear existence; there is no time in spirit.

One night the phone rang at about 9:00. I put down the astrology book I was engaged in and headed to the kitchen. I glanced at the caller ID and saw it was Rick's number. It had been six weeks since we'd spoken. My heart stopped for a moment, and then I picked up the phone.

"Hello," I answered.

"Hi, it's Rick," he said, sounding upbeat but nervous.

We spoke for awhile, exchanging surface conversation. Neither of us bought up issues from the past. We acted as if nothing needed to be resolved—like old friends catching up.

"I'm moving out of town in a couple of weeks and want to meet for dinner to say good-bye," Rick finally confessed.

Hesitant to accept the invitation, I took a deep breath and kept silent.

Rick seemed to feel my trepidation and said, "We could meet for a drink instead?"

I felt a quick drink would be safer, so I said, "Okay. I have an hour between work and bowling this Thursday."

"Great! I look forward to seeing you," Rick gladly exclaimed. We agreed on a meeting place and ended the conversation cordially.

After hanging up, I looked up at the astrological calendar positioned by the phone and noticed it was a full moon. That explained why Rick had called. In astrology, the moon is the ruling "planet" for the zodiac sign of Cancer, which Rick and I shared. Full moons symbolize the ending of cycles, and they often draw people out of their shells.

That Thursday, I walked into the restaurant and saw Rick having a drink at the bar. He looked up and spotted me, then smiled. When I walked over to him, Rick stood up, and we embraced.

"It's so good to see you. You look great," Rick gushed.

"Thanks. You look great yourself," I responded.

Our meeting went well. Rick spoke with excitement about the new chapter in his life. He was moving across the country and starting his own business. The time flew by. When the evening ended, we paid the tab and walked out to the parking area, hugged, and said good-bye. I drove to my bowling league with bittersweet feelings. I still didn't understand why we had been brought together, but I was happy to have loving closure for this relationship.

In July, Alexis; her fiancé, Jake; and I took a ten-day vacation to New England. We traveled through Maine, New Hampshire, and Massachusetts and ended our trip in New York. The trip was healing for me, especially the three-day visit to Acadia National Park in Maine.

I meditated on the peak of Cadillac Mountain, and it was a true spiritual experience. The mountaintop temperature was a brisk fifty-five degrees with a twenty-five-mile-per-hour wind. I wore blue jeans and a thin long-sleeved purple shirt. I sat in the lotus position and allowed the cool wind and clouds to blow across my body. I closed my eyes, inhaled through my nose, and exhaled through my mouth. The breeze chilled me to the bone, but moments of the sun's warmth restored my peace. I asked the universe to download any knowledge through the top of my head, my crown chakra. I eventually zoned out and felt centered; I didn't notice the weather any longer.

When I opened my eyes, I felt blessed and still. I looked around and saw the beauty. The plants and trees swayed with the wind, bending with such flexibility. *Can it be that humans must learn to do that same?* I wondered. *Maybe I need to continue to flow in the direction I'm blown; it's easier and wiser not to resist.*

I flew back to Florida and enjoyed the rest of the summer. Several long-distance friends visited, and we spent a lot of time at the beach.

One Saturday afternoon, Brock called.

"How's it going?" he asked.

"Great! I went on a New England vacation last month with Alexis and Jake. How's your summer?"

"I've seen many live concerts, and the weather has been great lately. I try to tan often—before fall comes around next month."

"How far do you think the Knicks will go this season?" I asked.

"I don't know—they seem unpredictable."

"Hey, how's the dating scene going?"

"Oh, I don't know," he said reluctantly. "It's been awhile. I'm looking for something more serious."

"You're an avid reader, so how about joining a book club to meet girls?" I suggested, feeling like his older brother.

"Maybe. It's an idea, I guess."

"Perhaps you can start your own club?" I suggested.

"That sounds better. I might consider it."

"Do what you enjoy, what you desire—eventually you will attract someone compatible to you," I offered.

"I'm ready to make a change," he confessed. "I need to open a new chapter in my life."

Brock talked about his struggle to move his life forward. I was glad he opened up to me, a sign that our friendship had deepened since his brother's death. We spoke for an hour and then ended our conversation, never knowing that it would be our last. It was late August 2001.

CHAPTER EIGHT

SHOCK

I will never forget that Tuesday morning. I woke to my alarm clock beeping at the usual time of seven. I shut off the alarm, recorded my dreams, and consciously thought about my day ahead. I'd registered to attend a small business seminar at nine that morning, so I was scheduled to work from noon until six. I had ample time before the five-mile drive to the hotel hosting the seminar, so I decided to lie in bed and watch television for a few minutes.

I surfed to the Weather Channel to see the day's forecast. The weather segment showed the New York City skyline from the New Jersey side. The camera captured a beautiful day with blue, sunny skies. I saw the Staten Island Ferry going across the harbor toward downtown and remembered taking that boat ride for ten years as I commuted to Wall Street. After the local Tampa forecast aired, I turned off the television and prepared my breakfast. The date was September 11, 2001.

The business seminar was free, so my mother, who had recently moved to Tampa, had signed up to attend with me. She and I entered the lobby at 8:55 and saw a crowd of people gathered around the television. I glanced at the screen and saw smoke coming out of one of the World Trade Center towers. Someone told me that a plane had crashed into one of the buildings. At first I thought it was a small aircraft that carried a handful of people. I said a quick prayer for those who had perished, and I walked away. Just two hours before, I had been watching the same panoramic view of New York on a beautiful day—and now it was broken by smoke and flames.

I registered and entered the workshop. An hour passed and then the mediator announced a fifteen-minute break. I stepped out of the seminar room, headed to the lobby, and saw an even larger crowd of people fixated on the television. I hurried over and was told that a second plane had crashed into the other tower. Seeing both buildings ablaze, I thought, *Oh my God, how could two accidents happen like that? The smoke of the initial crash probably obstructed the view of the second small aircraft, causing it to crash.*

The crowd around the television stood in utter disbelief. I overheard someone mention that this was an act of terrorism and that the planes were hijacked commercial airliners. How anyone could commit such a heinous act was beyond my comprehension. I flashed back to the car bombing of the World Trade Center in 1993. I worked on Wall Street then, and at the time, I thought the attack was a disaster of epic proportions. But this already seemed much worse.

Feeling sad and concerned, my mother and I decided to abandon the next segment of the seminar. Mother felt anxious and worried about Alexis, who worked in New York City. I didn't have a cell phone, so we drove back to my home to call Alexis.

In the car, we listened to the disaster coverage on the radio. Mother cried and grew more anxious, which made me anxious. When we arrived home, Mother turned on the TV, and I went into the kitchen to call Alexis. I couldn't get through; all the phone lines were busy. I decided to take the rest of the day off and called into work. My coworker then informed me that Alexis had called to say that she was okay.

After I hung up, I ran to the TV and witnessed the first tower collapse. Mother and I watched in shock, with tears of disbelief pouring out of our eyes. When the second tower fell, I felt I was losing people I knew. I couldn't remember exactly who worked in the towers or the surrounding buildings—or if they'd moved locations, as companies do so often.

Then the phone started ringing, and it didn't stop all day. I received calls from ex-lovers and old friends trying to find out if my family members in New York were okay. While the images of destruction replayed over and over on the television screen, I talked on the phone with nearly everyone I knew, trying to make sense of what had happened.

At 6:00 p.m., I received a call that rocked my core.

I answered, and a worried female voice blurted out, "Marty, I think God took Brock."

Speechless for a moment, I finally recognized the voice as Molly's, Brock's mother's. "Are you sure?" I asked.

"He worked in one of the towers."

I thought for a moment and remembered that he did work at the World Trade Center. I then got a sinking feeling in my gut.

"Oh my God," I said.

Molly was beeped for another call and placed me on hold. While I waited, I thought about what this time must be like for Molly. She had just buried Luke, Brock's older brother, three years earlier. I couldn't imagine her difficulty in losing her second and last son.

She clicked back and said, "Marty, I need to keep a line open just in case he's injured or stuck somewhere."

"I'm praying for you," I said. "Please keep me posted. I love you." And I hung up.

I walked to my living room and paced for half an hour in utter disbelief. I felt deep in my gut that Brock had died. I couldn't eat dinner. I lit a candle, prayed, and watched TV until midnight.

The next few days were a blur. I went into work, but each day we were sent home early. At home, I watched TV and waited for news of survivors like everyone else in the world. I didn't want to give up hope that somehow I might be wrong about Brock's condition.

I called Molly daily to check up on her, but she still had no news. She was in constant contact with Brock's roommate and biological father in New York. All she could do was hope and pray. As the days went on, her energy slowly drained, and so did mine.

A few days after the attacks, I hit a breaking point. Drained and stressed, I needed to detach from all the drama and mass panic. I didn't want to watch television anymore. So I worked, ate, spoke on the phone, and read books for a week.

I came to accept that Brock had died. I decided to do something constructive with my grief. Since I hadn't decorated much since purchasing my condo, I decided to feng shui my home. *Feng shui* is Chinese for "wind and water." It's an ancient Chinese art of harnessing positive energy to enhance abundance and love through the proper placement of elements and colors in the home. I hired a practitioner to give me suggestions for my residence. During the three-hour consultation, I received many helpful hints to create peace, harmony, and auspicious energy.

For the next month, working full-time and decorating my home became my focus and salvation. I listened to music to keep me inspired and to aid my continued healing. Brock and I had loved the song "Black" by Pearl Jam, so I included it in my playlist. The first time I hit Play on the random shuffle, "Black" was the first song to come up. I took this as a sign that Brock was somehow all right. I stopped cleaning and paid silent homage to my lost friend.

For the first five weeks after September 11, Molly and I spoke for two hours every night. I found her strength remarkable. Taking one day at a time, she slowly accepted the fact that Brock was dead. His body was never recovered.

Then on the morning of October 16, 2001, I had the following dream:

I was standing in a dark room. I saw Brock within a tall block of glass. I was glad to see him. I asked if he was okay and if he'd made it to the other side. He looked up at me, seeming dazed and confused, and said, "I feel like I was in a dream, but I am waking up now."

As soon as I woke up, I recorded the dream and then recorded my first conscious thoughts:

> I feel like Brock is alive and well spiritually. But I believe he is in the middle of two worlds. I do not feel that he is earthbound, but in a cocooned stage—still in transition. The impression I got from the dream was that he was transitioning from unconscious to conscious. Could it be that Earth is the illusion and the spirit world the reality? I know this was a real spiritual visit because I took my current level of consciousness to this dimension.

I called Molly right away, "Hi, its Marty," I began. "Are you sitting down?"

"Yes," she replied. "Tell me what's wrong."

"I visited Brock last night in my dreams."

"Oh my God. Where is he? Is he okay?"

I shared my dream. Molly got so excited—she thought the dream meant that Brock was alive.

"I wonder if he's laid up somewhere, still unidentified?" she said. "Maybe he came to you in a dream to tell you."

I kindly told her what my more realistic thoughts were.

A week later Molly prepared two celebrations to honor and memorialize Brock's life: one in New York and one in Florida.

The dream about Brock helped me achieve further closure from that terrible day we now call 9/11. I felt grateful for the ten years of friendship and the numerous memories that Brock and I shared. Thanks to my dream, my conscious life was a bit more bearable. I felt more empowered to assist Molly during her time of need.

I accompanied her to New York for the celebration of Brock's life. We shared meaningful conversation on the flight. Once we landed, I noticed that her energy level had dropped significantly, and her eyes welled up. The enormity of the situation had taken its toll. I held her hand and slowed down to match her walking pace as we slowly deplaned. My heart went out to her.

At the hotel in Queens where we were staying, I wheeled our luggage while Molly checked us in at the front desk. In the elevator, Molly handed me the room keys. I asked her which room number she wanted. She told me to decide—it didn't matter to her. I added the room numbers to come up with a single digit. One added up to 8 and the other to 9. In numerology, Molly's life path number is an 8 and mine is a 9. I made my decision based on that.

We entered her room first. Molly immediately sat down and searched her purse for her sister's phone number. As I wheeled in the last of her luggage, I fixated on the painting hanging over her bed. It depicted the New York City skyline, including the Twin Towers, on a sunny day. My eyes grew wider when I noticed a plane in the upper left corner flying towards the towers.

I immediately looked away so as not to draw attention to it. *Did I make the wrong decision about our rooms?* I wondered. I became unglued for a moment, but then I gathered my senses and offered to assist her with anything else. She wanted to unpack and settle down, so she urged me to check into my room. I told her I would stop by in half an hour and left.

My room had no paintings of New York, but I wondered if similar paintings of the skyline were scattered throughout the hotel. I went back to Molly's room as planned. She seemed unaware of the painting. I sat on a chair facing it, and she sat on the bed facing me. I kept staring at the art, wondering about the "coincidence." Then the thought hit me: *The painting has to be a sign that Brock is with her.* As we reviewed our agenda for the three-day visit, Molly made it perfectly clear that she didn't want to set foot in New York City, especially not Ground Zero.

We honored Brock's life with family and friends in Queens. Molly released two balloons in honor of Luke and Brock. Molly's spirits seemed to lift with the support of so many of Brock's friends.

I had purchased a large journal so everyone in attendance could document a special memory or convey a message to Molly. It was a beautiful day, and the heartfelt eulogy brought tears to everyone listening.

While leaving the memorial, I bumped into Brock's ex-girlfriend from years past who worked for the same company as Brock. She said, "I was getting ready to head for work on 9/11, but my fifteen-month-old son developed a high fever due to his molars coming in, so I called out sick since I couldn't drop him off at daycare." That story and countless others like it profiled in the news had me thinking that a script—fate—was unfolding, that those who were delayed or forced to skip that workday had been destined to be elsewhere. We flew back to Florida and continued to heal.

The holidays were already fast approaching. I flew back to New York for Christmas, and Aunt Nancy and I ventured into Manhattan and visited Ground Zero for the first time.

It was a typical chilly, damp, and drizzly New York winter day. As we approached Ground Zero, I felt the enormity of the disaster as far as three blocks away. Many were trying to see the site, but it was closed off from public view. We advanced as far as civilians were allowed and stopped to watch the crew work. Down the street to my right, a flat truck headed toward me carried a large steel beam with a four-foot bolt sticking out of it. *How could such a strong structure bend*? I thought with amazement. It was my first up-close view of the debris. I quickly snapped a photo and indelibly imprinted the image in my mind.

Two days after Christmas, on what would have been Brock's thirty-second birthday, I flew back to Florida to be with Molly. She had planned to celebrate his birthday with a holiday gathering at her home. I stayed a couple of days, and then before heading back home to ring in the New Year, she gave me a Christmas gift: a porcelain trunk with Psalm 23 inscribed on the lid: "He leadeth me beside the still water. He restoreth my soul."

I was astonished. This was the second message I had received to read that quote. I told Molly that Mike, the psychic, had told me to read it months earlier. Molly said that she had purchased three porcelain trunks, all with different biblical quotes, and had decided to give me this one. I knew it was a divine sign informing me of my spiritual mission.

The end of the year at the bank was always very stressful, as many corporate clients wanted their demands executed before the New Year. This year, I experienced light-headedness at work. This alarmed me, so I took additional vitamins and drank more water. One morning, I stepped on my home scale and realized I had lost more than thirty pounds that year. The mental and emotional roller coaster had deeply affected me physically.

After the holidays passed, I read my astrological forecast for the coming year and looked at an ephemeris to gauge the speed of the planets in the solar system. I had one more year to complete my transformation cycle. My forecast indicated that the next part of this astrological event promised a "birth." Having survived an unbelievable 2001, I couldn't believe what would take place in 2002.

CHAPTER NINE

SURREAL

Molly called one evening and asked if I would accompany her on an impromptu trip to New York. Her request seemed odd—ever since the terrorist attacks, she had expressed immense displeasure at the idea of visiting New York.

She explained, "While watching TV, a clip of the attacks aired, and I saw the buildings fall. I was caught off guard. Then suddenly, I felt the desire to go to Ground Zero. Maybe if I confront the battleground, it won't have power over me anymore. Also, I saw firemen working at Ground Zero throughout the Christmas holiday, and I would love to visit a fire station to hug and thank them."

I agreed to accompany her on this healing mission. Molly, a friend of Brock's, and I flew into New York on a Friday evening. On Saturday, we rented a car and drove toward Ground Zero. Because of the weekend traffic and crowds, it took an hour to drive a few miles from midtown to downtown. The closest parking garage was a few long blocks from Ground Zero. Molly wanted to park closer, so we inched along in traffic.

After being stuck at a standstill only three blocks from Ground Zero for fifteen minutes, Molly insisted, "We'll find parking on this street." I thought it was wishful thinking—I had worked in the area for ten years and knew that street parking was a nightmare. But as we slowly rolled toward the end of the block, a delivery truck miraculously pulled out right in front of our car, opening a parking space. I grabbed the spot right away. After parking, I looked at Molly and said, "It's a sign that Brock is with us." She agreed.

We first walked to a nearby fire station so Molly could hug a fireman. I asked to use the bathroom and was escorted to the back. Upon my return, I noticed the firemen still wore the shock of the disaster on their faces. They graciously spoke with us for twenty minutes, openly expressing their sadness and disbelief. As I listened, I looked into their eyes and saw a beautiful, loving soul in each man. We then said our good-byes and headed for the huge task of viewing Ground Zero.

About a block from the site, we passed a church with prayers and statements plastered all over its black iron entrance gate. We stopped to read them, and grief overwhelmed me. I wanted to cry, but I wanted to be strong for Molly, so I stopped reading the memorials and detached emotionally. We continued on in silence.

Once we arrived at Ground Zero, we saw a long line of people waiting to view the site. The line looked endless; there must have been thousands waiting. I walked up to a bystander and asked whether we could enter the viewing platform. He told me that we needed to get a ticket and then go all the way to the end of the line.

I went back to where Molly was standing and told her what we had to do. She looked over at the police officer manning the metal barricade blocking the entrance ramp. "Follow me," she said. "I have a gut instinct."

Molly said to the officer, "My son died here on September 11. I just flew in from Florida and would appreciate if we could enter the viewing platform without waiting on the long line."

Without hesitation, he turned around, moved the metal barricade, and allowed us in. As we entered, I turned to see how the other people waiting reacted to the officer's good deed. There was no reaction—everything was peaceful, as if the three of us were transparent. I knew it was another divine sign from Brock.

We walked the five hundred feet up the ramp to the viewing platform. Shock, awe, and respect filled the air. After what felt like an eternity, we finally reached the front. We took a breath and gazed at the site.

We stared at a huge pit. It had been four months since the attacks, and miraculously, most of the debris had been cleared. The surrounding buildings looked exposed and vulnerable, lonely for the tall neighbors that had protected their facades for so many years. The sun had now set, and the twilight provided the backdrop for what looked like a peaceful end and a promising new beginning.

We found the site hollow but comforting. There were no tears, just gratitude that we were present at Brock's resting ground. In respect and acknowledgement, we stayed for ten minutes, and then we turned away to leave.

We were one block from the car when I heard coins fall to the ground in front of me. I looked down and saw pennies on the ground. I looked up to see if someone had dropped them from a window, but there was nobody around. I asked a woman who had just passed me if she had dropped any coins, but she said no.

I picked up the pennies, looked at Molly, and said, "We just received another divine message that Brock is okay." We hugged and laughed all the way to the car. Our healing mission accomplished, we flew back to Florida the next day.

Back in Tampa, I continued to deepen my work with astrology. I frequently visited my favorite astrology website to learn about past-life karma and abandonment issues. I ordered practically every report available. But when I came across the Compatibility Report for Lovers, I hesitated. It required that I provide birth data not only for myself, but also for my romantic interest.

On Valentine's Day, the website offered the report for half price. On previous Valentine's Days when I was single, I would cook a candlelight dinner for Cashmere and me and allow her to eat on top of the dining room table. But this year was different: I had no lover, and my cat was dead. I had neither seen nor spoken to Rick in months. Although I no longer pined for him, he had been my last romantic interest. I decided to indulge and humor myself by ordering the report. I populated the birth data for Rick and me and printed the report.

While reading about the planetary aspects that described our strengths and weaknesses in a partnership, I had a profound realization. One of the planetary aspects, which included the planet Pluto and the moon, indicated that Rick and I had shared a tumultuous past life together. The next sentence provided the epiphany I needed: "We agreed to work out our past life emotional connection in this lifetime." It all made sense. My feelings for him were the strongest I'd felt for anybody. He had been my obsession for the better part of a year. Although I felt our encounter had been scripted, I didn't know why I had loved and hated him so deeply. I couldn't run away from our relationship, either—I had no place to hide. We were guided to work out our *emotional* agreement.

In addition to the obligation, I also felt intuitively that Rick was my mirror for both my strengths and weaknesses. And to fall in love with someone who was born the same day and year as me could not have been a coincidence. This confirmed the mirror idea.

I said a prayer and hoped that our shared karmic obligation had been completed in this lifetime. I never wanted to relive such emotional intensity in an intimate union. I chalked up the obligation to another divine lesson along the train tracks of knowledge.

Soon after, I received a surprise phone call from my old friend Tony. He had just relocated to Florida from New York with his wife, Liz; their two boys; and his father, Tony Sr. I'd attended his wedding many years before and had maintained a relationship, speaking to him and his family about once a year. I'd never felt comfortable telling them about my sexual orientation. When Tony invited me over for dinner to reconnect and catch up on our lives, I felt obligated to accept the invitation to welcome them to Florida.

As I drove over to Tony's home for dinner, I knew I would be probed about my intimate life. I recounted many occasions in New York when Tony Sr. would ask, "Marty, you're a good-looking guy; why aren't you dating any girls?" I always responded, "I'm too busy with work and school to date anyone." This time, if they asked, I would tell them I was gay. I had made a commitment to myself to live in truth every day.

I arrived with an apple pie for the adults and toy trucks for the boys. All gave me a wonderful greeting, and then I received a tour of their new house. When we were ready to sit for dinner, I excused myself to wash my hands. I looked into the bathroom mirror and said, "Okay, God, it's showtime. This is going to be a most interesting dinner."

I sat down, and we passed around the spaghetti and garlic bread. After some small talk, Tony Sr. asked, "Hey, Marty, are you dating anyone?"

"No, not right now," I replied.

"How long have you been living in Florida?"

"Five and a half years."

"Five and a half years!" he exclaimed. "That's a long time! How come you're not dating?"

"Well, I've dated since I moved here, but I'm currently single."

"How old are you?"

"Thirty-three," I replied.

"Marty, you're a good-looking guy. I bet you attract a lot of women. When are you going to marry and have kids?"

I politely chewed the mouth full of spaghetti while he waited for my answer. After the pause, I confidently said, "Actually, Tony, I date men."

The room went silent. Even the fifteen-month-old stopped babbling in his high chair and looked at me.

Tony Sr. fired back, "Marty, listen to me! You don't have to tell anybody about this! It's nobody's business! You hear me?"

I wondered, *Why is he yelling at me? Is he angry at my admission or trying to protect me?*

"Yes, I agree. It's nobody's business," I said.

Tony Sr. then changed the topic by asking if I liked the spaghetti. Tony and Liz continued eating as if nothing had happened. Tony slurped his spaghetti, letting marinara sauce drip from his chin As I looked around the room, I felt relieved and weird at the same time. An uncomfortable silence came over us. I asked Liz about her pregnancies and childbirth experiences, and she elaborated on both events for ten minutes. She then excused herself to attend to the children. I continued the flow of conversation by asking Tony about his new job. The dinner table was then cleared, and we prepared for dessert.

During dessert, I shared the dream I had about Brock and mentioned that his mom, Molly, and I found comfort in dreams and other signs from the afterlife. Liz, whose mother had died from cancer a year before, spoke about how she missed her mother terribly but often felt her presence.

The conversation about death, healing, and signs from the afterlife continued for three hours. Everyone opened up about their losses and their experiences. The energy was beautiful. Tony Sr. shared stories of signs and dreams from his deceased mother and his wife, Tony's mother. I especially enjoyed a particular story he told about a couple that had to put their sick dog to sleep. The day after the dog's death, the couple woke up to laundry scattered on the bedroom floor. They were shocked but knew the mess had been left by their dog in spirit, as he had scattered their laundry all the time when he was young and healthy. They took this as a sign that their dog was young, healthy, and happy again in heaven.

We ended the evening around midnight. The kids were asleep on the living room couches. We exchanged good-byes and made plans to meet again in the near future. As I drove home that evening, I felt happy and peaceful. I was amazed at how open everyone had become when I'd steered the conversation toward spiritual matters. I now looked at Tony and his family with more love and less judgment. The evening renewed my faith in truth and love.

I realized that when I judged Tony and his family, or anyone in my life, my ego was engaged. Now that I was more conscious, more spiritual, it had become clear that everyone is created equal. We all hurt regardless of our economic or academic backgrounds. We are not immune to loss and pain, and more importantly, we're able to heal.

Right around the time of the dinner, I noticed that during my regular phone conversations with Molly, my cordless phone went dead within the first few minutes. I thought that was strange, because I always kept the phone on its charger, and it was usually fine, even when I talked for over an hour at a time to someone else. I purchased a new battery, but even after it was fully charged, the phone still went dead every time I talked to Molly. It didn't even beep to signal a low battery level—it just stopped working. Luckily, I also owned a conventional corded phone, for hurricane emergencies, so I'd switch to that phone to complete our conversation.

Then I would get a vision that the phone battery was low and going to die again—and in seconds, it would. After a month of these occurrences, I finally realized that Brock was manipulating my battery whenever I spoke with his mother. When I finally acknowledged his presence out loud, the cordless phone stopped dying. I joked to Molly, "Your son is costing me money. He owes me for a new battery."

Molly called one day to surprise me with an invitation to accompany her on an Alaskan cruise. She'd often told Brock that she'd always wanted to visit Alaska, and she wanted to treat me for assisting her throughout the ordeal of losing him. I was shocked and grateful, and I gladly accepted her gift. I looked forward to our departure in late June.

During a holistic expo in April, I ran into Carol, the aura photographer. I had just read *Many Lives, Many Masters* by Brian L. Weiss, MD, and told Carol I wanted to have a past-life regression. She said that she'd been through them many years before and that they'd helped her quite a bit. Carol's past-life-regression therapist happened to live in my neighborhood, so she gave me the therapist's name, Janet, and contact information.

A week later I called Janet and scheduled a session for the following week. When I arrived for my appointment, Janet introduced herself and led me to a sitting area for our initial consultation. I liked her presence from the moment we met. She had a sensitive, strong, and compassionate spirit. To my delight, she was also a Cancer. We were very receptive to each other. I knew this was going to be an eventful session.

After the consultation, we entered the regression room. I lay down on what looked like a massage table, and she guided me through a meditation. I was so relaxed that I couldn't feel my body. Janet then took me through a tunnel, and within seconds, I went back to a lifetime in Mexico in the late 1700s. Alexis was my sister in that lifetime as well, which confirmed what many regression therapist had said: that we incarnate as a soul group. I had suffered abandonment in that lifetime as well: my mother and father had died while I was young. I'd had to develop courage and independence. After a long life, I had died peacefully in my sleep. Interestingly, I had always felt that I would die in my sleep in this lifetime. I didn't know if that was a memory from that lifetime or a premonition for this one.

I drove home after the session having learned that we repeat themes in each lifetime. It made sense—it would be difficult to perfect a theme in one lifetime, and obstacles similar to those I'd encountered in the past had surfaced in my current lifetime. This truth elevated my consciousness and gave me additional confidence to navigate my life more effectively.

Two days before my Alaskan cruise, I realized that my passport had expired the month before. I didn't have time to renew it before we left, so I decided that when the ship docked in Canada for a day, I'd stay on board. Since Molly had booked the cruise, I called her to make sure I didn't need a passport to board the ship.

She read the documents and called me back. "Just bring a valid picture ID. No passport is needed." I thought that was strange, because of the scheduled Canada stop, but I packed my driver's license with my luggage and assumed the matter would be closed.

I arrived at Molly's the evening before our flight, and she gave me my cruise package, which included my ticket and other information. I read everything and found that not only did I need a valid passport or birth certificate to enter Canada, but I also needed one of these documents to board the ship. My excitement quickly turned to disappointment. I didn't have enough time to get my birth certificate and fly out the next morning, and I had just worked a full day, driven four hours across the state, and was exhausted. Molly apologized for misinforming me but guessed that I would be okay boarding anyway. I thought that unless she had some clairvoyant insight, her confidence was unrealistic. Despite my trepidation, I went to sleep and hoped for a miracle.

I had a good night's rest and woke up feeling good. I showered, ate, and headed to the airport with Molly. We flew to Seattle, Washington, where the ship was departing. Molly's sister, Shelly, flew in from New York and joined us for the cruise.

Once inside the cruise terminal, we passed through the first of two identification checks, and only a picture ID and the ticket were required to pass. I was relieved to get through, but as we walked toward the boarding area, I saw a long line before us. We took our place at the end, and I saw a sign that indicated that a passport or birth certificate must be accompanied by a valid picture ID and cruise ticket in order to board. *Security is really tight since 9/11,* I thought. *How are they going to allow me to board without my birth certificate or US passport? I'm going to be stuck in Seattle.* I stood on line for thirty minutes, wondering what my fate would be.

We finally reached the front of the line and were summoned to the check-in seating area. All three of sat behind a large table, and the sweet lady sitting opposite said, "Please take out your documents and IDs. We need to photocopy them for our records." Shelly was seated to the left, Molly in the middle, and I to the right. The lady typed our names on her computer while we gathered our documents. I held out my boarding ticket and driver's license, hoping for a miracle. What happened next astounded all of us.

The lady looked up, took Shelly's and Molly's documents, and said, "I'm going to step away to photocopy these. I'll be right back." I sat bewildered, unsure of what had just happened. It was almost has if I had become transparent for a moment. The woman neither looked at me nor requested my documents. I put my license and ticket in my shirt pocket and sat quietly. The lady came back and handed over the originals to Shelly and Molly, and then another officer manning the check-in line distracted her with a question. Once she had finished speaking to the officer, she directed her attention back to us.

She looked at me in confusion and asked, "Did I copy your information?"

Molly immediately responded, "Yes, you did."

The lady then smiled and said, "Thank you. You can now board the ship."

I stood up, and Molly and I smiled at each other. We had just witnessed divine intervention. I didn't draw attention to the miracle that I had prayed for. I picked up my luggage and headed to the X-ray machine. Once our bags were cleared, we boarded the ship.

We went to our cabins, unpacked, and met back at Molly's cabin. Molly unpacked a small bottle of grape juice and plastic champagne glasses, and we toasted our voyage. We all spoke about the miracle and had a feeling that this cruise was going to be magical.

We enjoyed the first couple of days at sea playing bingo, sitting in the sun, exploring the ship, and taking in the evening shows. On the third day, Molly, Shelly, and I went on a whale-watching excursion. We videotaped whales, sea lions, and sea otters frolicking in the ocean.

On the fourth day, I met Molly in her cabin to review our itinerary for the day. We were seated on opposite sides of her bed reading the scheduled events when I noticed that the lights over her vanity were blinking, and I pointed this out.

"Yes, I know." She sighed. "I reported it to maintenance yesterday. They checked it out and couldn't find the cause. They even tested the electricity running through the adjoining cabins and changed the lightbulbs."

A few minutes later I noticed the lights in the hallway near the entrance of her cabin started to blink. I brought that to Molly's attention, and she commented, "Oh, maybe my children are here." For the next minute, I focused on the area between the vanity and the hall lights. I tried to see if there was any rhythm to the blinking but did not find one. Then, incredibly, the lights above the bed started to blink. Molly stopped reading and joined me in amazement.

"I feel like this experience is right out of a movie," I commented.

"This is so surreal," she said, looking astonished.

The incredible amazement continued.

"Is that you, Luke, Brock, Mom, and Dad?" Molly said out loud. "If so, blink once for no, twice for yes."

The lights over the bed stopped completely and then blinked twice.

"Oh my God," I gasped, almost falling off the bed.

Molly continued, "Will I remarry?"

Once again the lights blinked twice. Molly joyfully yelled, "Yeah, I'm going to be in love and wed again!" We both laughed out loud. Shelly then knocked on the door, and we shared our experience with her. It was raining that day, so all of us decided to walk around town and shop for the day.

The next morning, day five, we met again in Molly's cabin. I decided to play back the videotape to see everything we had recorded. The tape rewound for only a few seconds and then started to play. I thought it was odd that it rewound that quickly after videotaping almost two day's events. When it started with only the previous day's activities, I realized that the whale-watching excursion was not there. Molly and I had taken turns with the video camera that day, and neither of us recorded anything. We had both made the same mistake of pushing the Power button but not the Record button. Molly was deeply disappointed.

I immediately picked up that day's event schedule and learned that there was another whale-watching excursion in the afternoon. I asked Molly if she wanted to go again if there were tickets available. She said, "Absolutely." I inquired, and they still had space available for that event. Molly purchased the tickets. We went on the trip and remembered to hit the Record button. This second whale-watching trip was even more incredible. We captured more whales and sea animals than in the previous excursion. We were so happy to have had another chance.

On day six, we docked at beautiful Victoria Island, Canada. I had wanted to visit this island ever since I'd missed out on seeing it during a minivacation to Vancouver a few years before. That morning, all the passengers received a notice under their cabin door saying that we'd have to pass through a passport check point before disembarking in Canada. It didn't discourage me though: divine intervention had pushed the envelope thus far, so I figured I might as well try Canada. It turned out my instinct was right: Dorothy and I quickly flashed our driver's licenses at the checkpoint and entered Victoria Island with no problems.

On our last night, we packed our bags and left them outside our cabin doors as instructed. The following morning, the cruise personnel took the bags off the ship. When we docked at the terminal, the personnel reiterated that we needed to show our passports to officials in order to disembark. When it was our party's turn to exit, Molly went in front of me and told the official that she and I had inadvertently packed our passports in our luggage. The officer asked for our names and birth dates. His computer confirmed that we had checked in, and he cleared us to leave.

A couple of weeks after the cruise, Molly phoned and told me that she was never charged for our second whale-watching excursion. I considered the magic that happened on this vacation the spirit of an Alaskan cruise.

The following week, Cashmere came to me in a dream: I followed her up a staircase, and at the top step was a gray female Persian. I picked her up in one hand, scooped up my Cashmere with the other, and walked down the staircase carrying them both.

When I woke up, I was amazed that I had dreamed of Cashmere again. It had been two years since she'd passed and last visited. My mother had just taken in a stray female gray Persian cat she named Ashley, so I reasoned that Cashmere was giving me a heads-up that Ashley was coming into my life. Indeed, twelve days later Mother visited and informed me that she had quit her job and was moving back to New York in a few weeks. She asked if I could keep Ashley. I marveled at the accuracy of the dream. I adopted Ashley that day.

When fall I looked forward to viewing a new TV show called *Beyond with James Van Praagh.* I taped it every day along with a weekly animal-psychic show to view when I came home from work. The shows fed my hunger for spiritual truth. That fall I set aside a special day in for meditating, cooking chicken soup, and watching both shows. I called it Mystical Monday and kept up the ritual until year's end.

On one Mystical Monday, I exited my meditation area and headed to the kitchen to make soup. It was a new moon in the sign of Scorpio—the detective of the underworld often affiliated with death and the afterlife—so my meditation session had been especially powerful. My awareness still elevated, I set about chopping vegetables. I felt my cat rub against my leg, but when I looked down, I didn't see anything. I stepped away from the kitchen and saw Ashley sleeping on the living room sofa. I knew then that Cashmere had visited. She had always loved when I fed her chicken.

In late October I traveled to visit my friend Jerry in Venice Beach, California. He had recently relocated there from New York. His sister, Rose, lived in Studio City, so Jerry organized for all of us to meet for lunch.

Rose was a sweet, soft-spoken, and inviting soul with a passion for animal rights. She belonged to many animal organizations and had traveled extensively to provide a voice for them. During our conversation, Rose spoke about how much she and her husband had been affected by the loss of a close friend on September 11. They had seriously considered moving to a more serene environment and had chosen to enjoy life daily.

I asked how her friend had died. Rose said, "She was on the plane that was hijacked from Boston heading to Los Angeles. It was the first plane that went into the north tower of the World Trade Center."

"I lost a close friend that day too," I said, amazed at the coincidence. "In fact, the plane carrying your friend killed my friend. Brock worked on the 101st floor, just above where the first plane hit." Our friends had both died instantaneously.

We found comfort in our shared losses. This was a cathartic lunch planned by the universe.

Later that evening Jerry and I stopped to check in on a senior couple. The husband was ninety-three years old, and his wife was eighty-nine. They had been married for sixty years. What we'd intended as a brief visit turned into a two-hour discussion about life. The husband struck me a as true sage. He bestowed a wealth of wisdom upon me, including that the most important aspect to living a healthy and long life was laughter.

He confessed that he had been stressed out as a middle-aged man with two sons and had felt pessimistic about life. Then one day he had a hearty laugh over a TV show and started to feel great. He then made the connection between laughter and health and was determined to laugh every day. That had been more than fifty years before. When Jerry and I finally departed for a late dinner, I felt that the purpose of my trip had been to meet Rose and this wonderful sage. I was elated and blessed to be in his presence.

On the six-hour nonstop flight back to Tampa, I pondered recent coincidences, especially those from the past two years. I realized they had all been beyond my control—they had been divinely scripted. *There are no coincidences,* I thought. I closed my eyes and viewed my childhood, especially the tremendous role of my parents, objectively and awakened to many truths.

Parents leave their imprints in our hearts and minds forever. Their conscious or unconscious actions underlie our lives' designs.

As I flew thirty thousand feet above the earth toward Florida, I finally realized that my parents had been my teachers. Their actions or lack thereof had forced me to learn important spiritual lessons.

Holding on to the pain of uncomfortable memories would keep me in a state of victimhood. I didn't want that. I needed to see myself as a student, not a victim.

First I put myself in my father's shoes and realized he had dealt with abandonment too—his mom and dad had not been stable during his early childhood. The cycle of abandonment continued when I didn't see him after the age of eight. My parent had been absent.

Then I put myself in my mother's shoes and saw a frightened girl who had grown up in an environment of fear and anger. She also went through abandonment, estranged from her family for twenty-two years. She'd had Alexis at nineteen and then had struggled to make ends meet as a single mother of two. She'd done the best job she could under enormous stress, and I was very grateful to her. This understanding taught me the real meaning of forgiveness.

I'd criticized them in the past for their awful choices that caused me such great pain. It had taken many years to realize that blaming my parents wasn't the answer—it only led to more pain, not healing. I forgave my mother for all the instability and forgave my father for being absent.

I was also impressed that my dad's absence forced me to look at the real truth: that I didn't need anyone's approval or love, because I already had it within me. My despair had actually been a lesson to go within and realize that I'd been made from love, the energy of God. My soul is God, so I'm part of, not separate from, this source. My spirit, not my body, is the real me. This insight was important for self-acceptance.

This understanding made me fall in love with my parents. I felt like a father wanting to protect his frightened little children and to let them know that they are loved. It had been a tough journey coming to this understanding, but it ultimately led to my liberation.

Only conscious love, an awareness of the spark of God within, could heal such anguish. But like many in the world, Mother and her family spoke of God from the perspective of separation. They never believed they were co-creators of their earthly existence—a part of, not separate from, God.

Their lack of inner connection, and my past lives in spiritual orders, made it very clear that I needed to stay grounded and connected to my real source of guidance, the spirit within.

I realized that when I become cognizant of an unhealthy generational pattern, I had the power to change it. I did have a choice to exercise my free will. I needed to become conscious of these unconscious behaviors because life is cyclical. I could only change what I acknowledged. What would be truly sad would be to consciously repeat a destructive behavior, attitude, or pattern. But with consciousness, I didn't have to suffer the sins of my parents or grandparents. I sighed and let go.

Then I envisioned all of my ex-partners and found the commonality among them as well—they all had abandonment issues. I'd never felt loved by my parents and had unconsciously sought to fill this need by attracting such partners.

If I were to experience a healthy and happy relationship, I realized, it was important that I heal from abandonment. I had learned a few signs of unresolved abandonment issues, including unstable relationships, especially physically intimate ones, and a tendency to leave relationships frequently.

Loss enables us to grow, to expand—it does not diminish our potential. We need not wait for losses to experience growth and expansion, but emotional pain can motivate us to let go and turn the page. Nothing is ever truly lost, because spirit is the only thing that's real—and since it's source energy, it's indestructible.

The body is our responsibility temporarily. Since it houses our spirit for a short time, it is wonderful to love and care for it with adequate sleep, healthy food, and positive thoughts and emotions. Our bodies are also a source of sexual pleasure, and that makes the earthly journey much more bearable!

It was now up to me to heal from the past once and for all. Living the life of a victim would make me powerless and angry at the world, but with the authentic power of consciousness, I would be able me to see the miracles that I had unconsciously manifested.

My astrological chart showed that childhood and parental issues were two opportunities I'd master. It was all in my script. My blueprint also showed that divine intervention played a critical role in my past and present incarnations. My script had been written for me to rely on the universe and not others' opinions. This awareness compelled me to show others how the universe is the true source of strength, but living with the new mind-set of truth took time to master.

My two-year astrological transit was coming to an end. I had been given so many revelations and transformations. I'd chosen to listen to these signs and stop resisting them, and in doing so, I'd learned the *real* meaning of free will. I had learned that the universe was set up to teach us, not to harm us. My life flowed when I embraced spiritual teachings.

I'd confronted my painful past, my karmic obligation. The pain gave way to healing, which gave way to liberation. The past was the key to my present and future freedom. The only tools I needed were courage, faith, and an open mind. My experiences had been scripted in my blueprint from my astrological past lives, but others wouldn't necessarily have to experience astrological transits to trigger these revelations.

Healing from pain and releasing blocks from the past allow us to live lighter, happier, and more fulfilling today. We all can do it!

My psychic gifts were alive and well, and my clarity constantly sharpening. Turmoil had a hidden blessing—that we are often most receptive to the universe during times of tragedy.

Throughout the rest of the year, I studied astrological charts from healers and spiritual authors. All featured Pluto prominently. Pluto transits had triggered similar experiences in these authors' charts and illuminated their spiritual missions. By divine order, I now attract many clients who are in a Pluto transit. I offer them guidance to embrace, not fear, this experience, as it is their passage to freedom.

After reading *The Lightworker's Way* by Doreen Virtue, PhD, I was guided to write this book. Now that I knew my mission as a healer, author, and spiritual teacher, only one question remained: how and when would I leave my well-paying job at the bank? I had one bigger test: to risk what I valued the most—domestic and career security. Would the universe reward me with more joy and abundance? I felt like a changed person, and I now knew that my mission was to educate others. I gathered some courage and made some bold choices.

CHAPTER TEN

LEAP

In January 2003, I requested two weeks' vacation from my job. I needed to slow down and value my precious time. During the respite, I stayed home. I felt peaceful and rested. My dreams were vivid, and I recalled one in particular:

I flew to a foreign country and then boarded a bus as the only passenger. The bus drove roughly through snow and mud, and at one point, climbed vertically up a mountain. It groaned as it struggled to reach the top. When the bus stopped, I stepped off and saw the most spectacular beach I'd ever seen. I felt I had reached heaven and was witnessing paradise. The colors were unbelievably vibrant. The water and sky shimmered in pure blue. People were swimming and having fun all around me.

When I woke up, I thought the dream signified that my journey to fulfill my spiritual mission would lead me to paradise. As symbolized by the bus ride along the rugged path, my road to success would not as smooth as I would have liked. However, if I stayed the course, I would ascend to my soul's fulfillment. The vibrant blue represented a spiritual teacher or guide.

That I was the lone passenger in my dream spoke volumes. All I needed to do was have the will to get on the bus and *enjoy* the ride and scenery—and trust that the universe would bring me to paradise. It was up to me to courageously leave my corporate job and its financial security and walk the solo path to freedom and glory. Psalm 23 entered my mind again: "Even though I walk in the dark valley, I fear no evil; for you are at my side with your rod and your staff that give me courage."

I started to write this book and build my media platform. I contacted a local spiritual publication that marketed my astrology business and asked if I could write an article on astrology, meditation, or dream analogy, subjects that I felt comfortable with. In reply, I received a list of topics that had been chosen for the publication for the entire year—none of them were the topics I'd requested. I read the submission guidelines anyway. I immediately felt that I was channeling writing angels who impressed me to write about one of the listed topics: the environment. The writing angels then gave me a creative idea about how to incorporate one of my own topics into the article. I thought about the inner and outer attributes one can develop to improve the environment on earth. I focused on recycling laws for the outer attribute and on meditation for the inner attribute.

I wrote and formatted the article and submitted it to the editor. After I sent the e-mail, a vision surfaced in my mind showing my published article and photo on the left hand side of a magazine spread. A week later I received an e-mail from the editor, who said he liked my article and was going to publish it. I felt elated! I looked forward to seeing my work in print for the first time.

Next, I focused on speaking engagements. I had received a postcard in the mail inviting me to the American Federation of Astrologers' summer conference in Arizona. My confidence was so high that I e-mailed the organization and requested if I could speak at the conference. After all, I had been a member for six years, graduated from the certification program, and purchased many astrology books from them. They graciously replied that they had already set the list of speakers but would add me to the reserve list just in case one of the speakers cancelled. I thanked them and continued knocking on doors.

Meanwhile, the spiritual signs from Brock were becoming increasingly obvious. During one of my monthly visits to Molly, while I waited for her in the living room, I heard a crash. I walked into the kitchen and saw a plastic Tupperware container on the tile floor. Someone (or something) had knocked it off the kitchen counter—but the room was empty. I acknowledged Brock's presence and laughed at his antics. I felt that he was thanking me for visiting his mom.

The following month's visit brought one of the most profound spirit encounters I've experienced to date. I was standing in the doorway of Brock's old room, which was the spare bedroom I slept in when I visited, and chatting with Molly, who stood about fifteen feet away in the kitchen. As we talked, I felt the area surrounding my body weightless. For a moment, I felt frozen in time. I was cognizant of my conversation but sensed that something or someone was next to me. A yellow shirt hung on a hanger on the doorknob, and as I turned my head to face the door, I saw the shirt flip through the air and land on the floor. I stared at it, dumbfounded. I couldn't believe it!

Molly asked what had happened, so I told her. She said she'd found the same shirt knocked to the floor the day before I'd arrived and wondered if it was a sign from one of her boys, likely Brock. I reassured her that she was right. She joked that the boys probably weren't happy with the way she'd ironed the shirt and were letting her know. We laughed about their mischievous natures and enjoyed a beautiful sunny day.

On the day my first article came out, I drove straight to the store and picked up a copy of the magazine. I opened it, looked in the table of contents, and saw my name listed. I picked up three additional copies and walked back to my car. I took a deep breath, opened to my article, and there it was—printed on the left-hand side with my photo as I'd envisioned. I read the article twice and felt proud all day at work.

I'd ordered tickets to attend a Sylvia Browne lecture with my coworker on the very day my article was published. I had attended one of Sylvia's public appearances two years before and knew about the lottery she offered for psychic readings. Upon arrival, each ticketholder received a plastic wristband with a raffle number printed on it, and a duplicate wristband was placed in a big bowl for the random drawing. Sylvia would lecture for the first hour, break for twenty minutes, and then do psychic readings the second hour, and the people whose wristbands matched the numbers she randomly chose from the bowl would have an opportunity to ask her one question. She usually picked about sixty numbers, and in a crowd of thousands, the odds of being picked were slim.

During the break, I got the same affirmative feeling I'd gotten during the James Van Praagh seminar, when I told Molly she would get messages from her deceased relatives. I prepared a question in my mind just in case my number was called.

After the break, Sylvia called out the first series of numbers, and just as I'd thought, I was chosen. I was seated on the second tier at the back of the crowded convention center, so the long walk up to the podium in front took forever. My heart was beating so fast I thought I would faint. I asked that angels to surround me and regained my composure. I lined up behind the other lucky audience members. Sylvia's assistant prepped us by making sure we had only *one* question prepared. He also instructed us to speak loudly and close enough to the microphone so that we would be audible on the recorded lecture.

When my turn came, I stepped up to the mike, and asked, "I'm writing a spiritual memoir and self-help book and wanted to know if I should self-publish or seek a literary agent for traditional publishing." I also snuck in another question: "Do you see the book doing well?"

Sylvia replied, "Please seek an agent. The book will be on the cutting edge of spiritual literature." I smiled and nodded in agreement. "It will do well," she concluded. I thanked her and felt elated as I made the long walk back to my seat.

My drive home from work was filled with joyful anticipation. I called Alexis in New York to share my experience. While chatting with her, I logged into my home computer to check my personal e-mails. I read a message from the American Federation of Astrologers advising me that a speaker had cancelled and that I would speak at the convention. I was so excited—three signs on the same day! I strongly felt that I was on the right path. The organization requested that I submit a synopsis of my lecture for their program within the week.

I submitted a quick synopsis of my presentation and used the six weeks before the conference to polish my lecture. I chose to focus on the planet Pluto and its healing effect. I incorporated many of the spiritual experiences that my clients and I had experienced during our Pluto transits.

On the plane ride to Arizona for the conference, I read a numerology book. I was amazed to learn that I was in the middle of a nine-year pinnacle cycle, learning attributes from the master number 11. This was a period of high sensitivity and intuition. The text also said that I would feel illuminated and transformed after the cycle ended. I calculated when this period began and realized that it had been when I relocated to Florida. It all made sense. I'd wondered why I had suddenly developed an insatiable appetite to read spiritual books and had been drawn to metaphysical studies since I'd moved.

On the opening night of the conference, a gathering was held for participants to register and mingle with other astrologers. After registering at the front, we were allowed into the ballroom, where seats had been assigned. I had been seated me at a front table with five other astrologers who were friendly but whom I didn't know. I was so focused on giving a good presentation that I failed to realize that they had authored books, were affiliated with various astrological organizations, and were prominent in their fields. So I learned a valuable lesson that night: I'd have to research other members prior to these conferences so I could network appropriately.

My lecture was scheduled for the first event in the morning of the following day. An hour before my presentation, I walked into the lecture room and mentally surrounded it with white light. I said a prayer for protection and courage and walked back to my room. I ate breakfast and meditated to relax. I reminded myself that nervousness was just energy that needed to be channeled. I returned to the lecture room ten minutes early so I could acclimate to the vibration.

Once people starting arriving, I broke the ice by chatting with those seated in the front. It relaxed me tremendously; I'd always felt more comfortable talking one-on-one or in small groups. I organized my papers behind the podium and waited a few minutes for the latecomers. Then I went for it. I opened the session with a meditation and continued with the ninety-minute lecture. Once it was over, I went back to my room feeling elated, on a natural high. I thanked the universe and the angels for their support and knew I needed to continue on this path.

During the rest of the conference, I met many interesting astrologers. I was drawn to one speaker in particular—an older woman who specialized in palmistry and astrology. After her lecture, I showed her my palms, and she pointed out specific lines in my right hand that meant I would change generational patterns and that my spiritual mission, or my life in general, would be intensified in this lifetime. She also said that I had incredible spiritual potential, indicated by a simian line, which joins the head and heart lines. I thanked her and felt her guidance to be true.

The last day of the conference happened to fall on my thirty-fifth birthday. The closing gathering took place in the early afternoon, so I made plans to drive up to Sedona and the Grand Canyon for the rest of the day. I couldn't think of a better birthday gift than to visit both majestic places. I had befriended a local gentleman named Randy who was also attending the week-long conference and was also on the spiritual path. He expressed a desire to accompany me on my birthday voyage, and I gladly accepted.

In Sedona we stopped to meditate at the vortex on Bell Rock. We separated to find our own places to sit and pray. Once I climbed to a place I felt guided to, I stopped and sat in the lotus position. I took a deep breath and felt chills run through my body. I sat still in total consciousness, feeling the energy from the vortex. I felt simultaneously intimidated and exhilarated. Once I'd relaxed I sent out my intentions for the upcoming year: courage to change my career, heal my finances, land a publishing deal, and have continued health for myself, my family, and my friends.

After our meditation, we headed to a local restaurant for a wonderful lunch. We stopped to take photos around Sedona and then headed north to the Grand Canyon. I enjoyed the entire ride from Scottsdale to the canyon. It was the first time I'd ever seen the desert and its many different cacti.

After checking into the lodge, we headed to the south rim of the Grand Canyon. I observed the stillness of the crowd as they allowed the magnitude of this Wonder of the World to penetrate their beings. The sun was setting, drenching the canyon walls in shades of terra cotta. The view was spectacular! It was a wonderful birthday experience. I stayed two more days, in which I took a couple of bus tours, and finally headed back home.

Meanwhile, as I was becoming more sensitive, my corporate job was becoming more of a burden. I struggled with the political environment and the heavy work volume. By the time I finished work and exercised at the gym to relieve my stress, I only had an hour or two to write. I needed more time to pursue my spiritual mission. I knew my career change was imminent, and I prayed for the day to arrive.

On the weekends I focused on my spiritual work and expanding my astrology business. The doors continued to open, letting me know I was on the right path. I e-mailed an editor from a free local news magazine to inquire about the price for placing a business card ad. When he found out I was an astrologer, he said he'd been looking for one to write a monthly column since his last astrologer had moved out of town. I informed him that I wrote monthly horoscopes for my website and could provide him with a link if he offered me free advertisement. He agreed, and we started a relationship.

One Saturday afternoon in fall, I was enjoying the cool weather flowing through the open windows of my home office. I stopped typing to breathe in the fresh air and felt elated to be at home writing. I was working on my book proposal and needed more time to complete it. *If I could work for organizations for the last eighteen years, why couldn't I give that allegiance to myself?* I thought. I contemplated my current financial obligations, which included a mortgage, car payment, utilities and other living expenses, and credit card debt. I decided to refinance my mortgage, which would allow me to pay off my car and create a small savings. I knew I could use funds from my 401(k) along with income from my astrology readings for living expenses for a few years. I would have to take the chance that my heart's desire and spiritual mission would provide the financial resources I'd need later in life. If I stayed at my job just to build my retirement account, I would die from stress before I could even reach senior age.

I looked at my astrology chart and mapped out a two-month period that would be auspicious for resigning my job and pursuing my career change. I wrote it all down and said a heartfelt prayer to the universe.

I wanted to further my momentum and desire, so I registered to attend a writer's conference in San Francisco and used the next two months to reach my goal of completing my proposal and pitching my book to interested literary agents.

I continued my spiritual momentum by attending an all-day seminar featuring four Hay House authors demonstrating their psychic abilities. I particularly looked forward to meeting Doreen Virtue. I felt such a connection to her teachings in *The Lightworker's Way*. The seminar was wonderful! I met Doreen at the book signing and found her physical presence just as beautiful as the messages in her books. She placed a bookmark inside my copy after she signed it. I thanked for her for work.

When I arrived home, I took out the bookmark and learned that she privately taught spiritual courses. A mediumship course caught my eye. The three-day course was taught in Laguna Beach, California, right after the writer's conference I planned to attend. *Is it a coincidence that I was already planning to be on the West Coast but haven't purchased my plane tickets yet?* I wondered. I had dreamt, felt, and smelled spirits around me for some time, but I needed guidance and confidence to sharpen my clairvoyant abilities. Again, I felt guided to study and learn, so I registered for the mediumship program and booked my flight for both events.

I had another month left before my projected resignation. During that time, I was summoned for jury duty. I was glad just to have a day off work. It was the first time I'd been called for this service, and someone told me to bring a book to read since the jury selection process would be long. I sat around in the waiting room and spent most of the day reading. When my name was called with a group of others, we entered the courtroom to begin the voir dire process: a preliminary Q&A session in which prospective jurors were questioned under oath to determine if they were suitable for the case.

The case we were being considered for involved a defendant charged with two counts of sexual molestation of a minor. After answering all the questions posed by the prosecution and defense attorneys, we were instructed to wait outside the courtroom while both sides chose the jury. While waiting, I had a strong feeling I would be chosen. After all, I didn't have children and had never been sexually molested, so I would be an objective candidate, and that made me favorable for both sides. After waiting twenty minutes, we were called back in, and my intuition was right again: I was chosen to sit on the jury of six—four women and two men.

As instructed, I arrived in court at eight o'clock the following morning. The jury members were all seated comfortably in the jury box, and the judge asked the state to start its case. During the prosecution's questioning of the first witness, one of the alleged sexual victims, something profound happened to me. The witness, a nine-year-old girl, was recounting what had happened to her on the day of the molestation, and a wave of anxiety came over me. I wanted to jump out of my own skin and out of the jury box. I was ready to stand up and yell, "Stop! I can't do this! I can't be here!" Then without warning, the feeling left me completely. I went back to being my peaceful and objective self, as I had felt when I started the day. *What the heck was that all about?* I wondered. *Did I just tap into the feelings the girl had at the time of her alleged molestation?*

The girl described that she was lured and touched by the defendant. Her testimony was compelling. She seemed so truthful and brave. After she finished, I listened to the next two victims, who had also allegedly been molested. Nothing psychic happened to me when they testified. However, we had been instructed to listen to the facts objectively and to reach a verdict based on the evidence presented.

During the lunch break, the jury was instructed not to discuss the court case among ourselves. So when we all piled into an elevator to head for lunch, everyone was quiet. To break the ice, I asked the other jurors their astrology signs. During lunch, I gave a few of them minireadings incorporating numerology and astrology. Everyone seemed receptive to this metaphysical lunch. It definitely took our minds off the sad testimony.

After the proceedings resumed and the last witness was called, we heard the closing arguments from both sides. Then the judge instructed us on how to deliberate, and the jury exited the courtroom. Once we were all seated in the deliberation room, we had to nominate a foreperson, and I was unanimously chosen. I wondered if my outspoken nature during lunch had convinced the other jury members that I would make a solid leader.

Then it hit me: the psychic experience I had earlier had forewarned me that I would be selected as foreperson, so I had needed to experience the girl's abuse in order to make sure that justice was served.

Now that we were behind closed doors, the women on the jury finally got a chance to express their feelings, and they really let loose, especially those who were mothers. It took an hour just to calm them down. I tried to appease them, but they were relentless. One of the mothers became indignant with me, yelling and accusing me of attempting to pacify her. I had no control over the process and seriously thought about forfeiting my new position. I detached from their emotional outbursts and stayed composed. Finally, one by one, everyone became more subdued and started to conduct themselves professionally. We discussed the trial in a civilized manner for the next couple of hours, making sure every voice was heard. We came up with a unanimous verdict.

We all held hands in a circle and said a prayer for the victims, the defendant, and our decision. I felt emotional, and two of the mothers cried. I rang the bell for the bailiff and announced that a verdict had been reached. After the verdict was read, I left the courtroom drained. The jury members said their good-byes, and we headed home.

The following month, I attended a wedding on the east coast of Florida. After dinner, a lady walked over to my table and sat down next to me. "You look familiar," she said. "Do you work for Nine Star Bank?"

"Yes," I replied, and I introduced myself. She told me she had worked for the same bank a year earlier but had left the job to start her own business. She was happier than ever and didn't regret her decision.

On my drive back, I thought about her words and found it odd that someone had recognized me three hundred miles away from home. I had worked for the bank the last fifteen years and had never seen her face. Part of me wondered whether she was a real person or an angel sent to give me a message.

During my lunch break one day, I made a deposit at another bank that housed my business account. It was out of my way, but I wanted to take a ride to clear my head from work stress. As I exited the bank, I was stopped by a police officer patrolling the entrance.

He asked, "Do you work for Nine Star Bank?"

I found his question puzzling at first, but I soon realized that he'd spotted the logo on the ID badge clipped on my shirt. "Yes!" I answered. "Why?"

"I worked for the same bank a year ago and left due to stress," he replied. "I passed the police exam shortly thereafter and became a patrol officer."

"Are you happier with your new career?" I asked.

"Elated," he replied.

We exchanged small talk and went our separate ways. The target date I'd set to resign was two weeks away, and I was clearly getting messages of encouragement.

A week before my target date, I was suddenly called into a late afternoon meeting. I double checked my e-mails and searched my desk for messages, wondering if I had been informed of this meeting earlier, but I found nothing. I sensed something covert was taking place and immediately asked for angels to surround me. When I walked into the meeting, a senior manager informed me that I was being removed from a major account that I had managed.

He said it had been a business decision that would benefit the bank and the relationship and that I would be reassigned to another account after the holidays. I accepted the news without being defensive. I humbly left the meeting and left for the day. On my drive home, I realized that this was my third sign to move forward with my career change.

I had picked the new moon, which symbolizes beginnings, to initiate my resignation letter and a full moon, which symbolizes endings, as my last day of employment. The night before I handed in my resignation, I asked the universe to give me a sign if I was making the wrong move: to either drain the battery from my car or make sure my home computer malfunctioned when I went to type my resignation. Part of me was scared to let go of a good salary and the sense of security it gave me—even if it was false, it was the only security I'd known.

The next morning, I woke feeling rested, powered on my computer without a hitch, and typed my resignation from my employer of fifteen years. When my car started, I knew this was really happening. I folded down my visor, looked into the mirror, and said the following prayer:

"God, today I resign my position created by man's ego and hire myself to work for you, through me, since we are one and the same. Amen."

I handed in my letter that morning. The next two weeks felt surreal. I was bombarded with visitors and e-mails asking if I was really resigning. To everyone who inquired, I repeated the same answers and never tired of the repetition. In fact, a natural high came over me each time I spoke. I felt like a spiritual presence was speaking for me, reassuring me in my decision with every encounter. Many wished me well and authentically believed that I would succeed.

As I drove to work for the last time, I reminisced about my tenure at the bank and the friendships I'd made in New York and in Florida. I shed tears of sadness and joy. I knew that letting go of this job would bring me much happiness. Now that I'd leaped, would the universe provide a safe landing?

CHAPTER ELEVEN

PATIENCE

I relished my newfound freedom. I had always wanted to take a nap every day, and now I could. I couldn't give my body the proper rest it needed before, especially midday, because of the full-time bank job. So now I created a balanced schedule with exercise, napping, writing, and astrological consultations.

Shortly after I resigned, I had the following dream:

I exited the grocery store and spotted a former coworker. She walked up to me and said, "Hi. How long has it been since you left the bank and started a new career?" I responded, "It's been one month." After a brief conversation, we exchanged good-byes and headed to the parking lot. As I approached my car, I noticed someone in the passenger seat. I couldn't see who it was, because it was dusk. I thought, *It must be my mother—she has a spare key to my car.*

I walked to the driver's side, opened the door, and leaned in to see who the passenger was. When he turned to face me, I saw that it was Brock. He looked into my eyes, and I was paralyzed with shock! I stared into his blue eyes in total awe of his presence. He then guided me to look at the floor below him, where he instantaneously manifested a basketball. He turned to me again and smirked. He was enjoying my shock response. He telepathically said, "Look at what I can do next!" and dematerialized before my eyes.

When I woke, I was amazed. Brock had shown me that he could manifest physical things with a thought. He wasn't constricted by the earthly laws; he was free to create and manifest with his mind. He looked so happy, and more importantly, I felt his soul was at peace.

I love that he had manifested the basketball, a symbol of our connection since we shared season tickets to the New York Knicks.

I also noticed commonalities with all his dreams:

First I was reassured that this dream was real through *current event confirmation*: when a scenario in a dream depicts an event that has recently taken place in the earth schoolroom. (It had been one month since my career change.)

Second, the spirit communicates telepathically. This form of spirit communication is the highest and most intelligent, given from consciousness to consciousness without interruption from the ego mind. The messages were clearly transmitted and easily absorbed. (I'd never seen a spirit open its mouth.)

The third point is the time of waking. I was awakened right after the dream so I could remember the amazing spirit visit. (Spirits typically visit right before you wake.)

I welcomed Brock's visits. He taught me more from the other side than he had when he was in physical form.

After this Brock dream, I completed my proposal and headed to San Francisco. I met many wonderful people, attended numerous writing classes, and received valuable advice from several published authors.

The last day included a "speed dating" event with literary agents in which authors had three minutes to pitch their proposals to each prospective agent. I practiced my book pitch and hoped for the best.

The speed-dating event was chaotic and crowded. The first two agents I met with rejected my pitch, so to sustain whatever confidence

I had left, I stepped outside to get some fresh air. I reconnected with my inner self and felt my confidence rise again. I headed back inside and sought out another agent.

But just before I spoke to a new agent, the organizers stopped the session for a bathroom break. Authors were instructed to stay in line or lose our spots. I had been having a spiritual discussion with a woman standing behind me, and when I turned around to resume our conversation, she started to cry. I sat her down on a chair, put my arms around her, and asked, "What's wrong?" She said, "My husband recently left me after seven years of marriage and I have felt shattered ever since. He's been verbally abusive lately. Now he's demanding a divorce."

I reassured her that she would survive the breakup and that it was all right to feel pain. I also told her that abuse in any form was not love and strongly suggested that she not tolerate it. I told her that with time, she would see this as a blessing in disguise.

"I prayed to God this morning and asked for a sign that I'll be okay," she said. "Now I know your words and support were God's answer to my prayers."

I continued to counsel her, and by the time the break was over, I was making her laugh. *I guess I needed to experience the rejections so I could be there for her, on that line, at that precise moment,* I thought. The next few agents were interested in my pitch, and I submitted my proposals to them.

On the last day of the conference, I woke up thinking about my ex-boyfriend Steve. I hadn't heard from or seen him since our tumultuous breakup four years before. An hour later I checked my e-mails and was surprised to see a message from him. He wanted to take me out for dinner so we could have a meaningful chat. I replied that I was out of town but that I'd e-mail him the week after I returned. Again, I was amazed at how receptive I was becoming. Picking up vibes had started to become second nature.

The next stop on my voyage was the mediumship class in Laguna Beach taught by Doreen Virtue. I slept soundly the first night. The morning of the first day of class, a new moon in the sign of Pisces, was peaceful. I knew it would be a magical day because Pisces is a sensitive and psychic sign. I ordered breakfast in my room and had no expectations about anything. After showering and getting ready, I made my way up to the top floor, where the seminar was being held. As I turned a corner, I passed a woman exiting her room. I quickly glanced at her and thought she looked like a goddess, with long flowing blonde hair, and sensed that she was a free and sensitive spirit. Within seconds, I heard footsteps behind me. I turned and saw that the goddess was Doreen Virtue. I immediately apologized for not recognizing her, and she welcomed me with a hug.

In class, Doreen guided us through a meditation to open our clairvoyance, our third eye, and asked that we document messages from spirits. Then we went around the room clockwise, listening to each student convey his or her message. Once a student spoke, the rest of us had to identify whether the message from the deceased person was affiliated with us. A pretty brunette opposite me conveyed a message from a female spirit who called herself "bright light." Nobody in the room could claim her. Doreen asked the speaker to garner another fact from the spirit. The student said, "Harriet."

I recognized the of an ex-coworker and raised my hand.

"Has Harriet passed over?" Doreen asked me.

"Not to my knowledge. She was alive at least a month ago," I said.

"Have your grandmothers passed away?"

"Yes. They have."

"What were their names?"

I was speechless for a moment. I'd never known my father's mother, so I didn't know her name, and I had suddenly forgotten my other grandmother's name. I sat and thought for a moment and then it hit me. "Luz!" I exclaimed. "Her name was Luz. Oh my God! Her name means 'light' in Spanish."

The students gasped in delight that we had finally identified the spirit.

"She's giving you her blessings and is handing you a broom," the student said. "She said she did this spiritual work before."

"Yes. My grandmother was a medium," I replied. "She held séances at her home."

"She's proud of you and wants you to succeed in this mission."

"Thanks, Grandmother. I appreciate your support," I replied.

Initially, I had thought that the broom Grandmother had sent me symbolized a good witch's broom. However, I later found out from Aunt Nancy that the broom actually symbolized my patron saint, St. Martin de Porres, known as "Martin of Charity," the saint of the broom, for his devotion to menial work. He's also known for his love of children and animals.

I learned a great deal that first day. Perhaps the most profound lesson was how deep and open my imagination were. I couldn't believe that the spirits had shown themselves to me and that I communicated with them telepathically. What I had thought was just my imagination was communication from actual people. They might be strangers to me, but they were true-life relatives of others. I found that Doreen's precise and sensitive teaching style resonated with my learning abilities.

During that first day, I met a woman named Becky who also lived in Tampa. We hit it off and became fast friends. I was amazed that in a class of only twenty-two people, I had met another person from the exact city I lived in. Doreen then ended the first day and instructed us to keep the same seating arrangement throughout the weekend seminar.

On the second day, I was last to enter the seminar and saw that someone was seated in my chair. Doreen's assistant immediately guided me to the seat next to Doreen's left and said, "This is your new seat for the rest of the seminar."

I sat down, and Doreen leaned over and quietly asked, "Was I in your dreams last night?

"I have no recollection of my dreams," I replied.

"You were in my dreams last night, and I wondered if you had a similar experience." She calmly smiled and began the day's lessons.

Doreen had us practice many readings with multiple classmates. We learned to see and communicate with spirits by keeping our physical eyes open and trusting the third eye. Doreen stood in the middle of the class giving us a demonstration for our next exercise, and when she walked to her seat, we both noticed a white feather that had magically appeared on her chair. We gasped in awe of the miraculous occurrence. Doreen showed the class, and everyone was astonished.

Our last day was even more compelling. For our graduation exam, we each had to stand alone, microphone in hand, and provide stage mediumship to other class members. I clearly understood how to trust my clairvoyant abilities, and I produced a wonderful message to a classmate from her deceased paternal grandmother. Doreen encouraged me to use my astrological background alongside mediumship when giving readings.

Once I completed my turn, I received my certificate, and I realized that all I needed to do was to trust the God Spark within me. The healing energy of the messages would take care of itself. After our graduation photo, we said our good-byes and headed home.

Back at home, I met up with Steve for dinner. It was strange seeing him after all these years. He hugged me hello, and we shared a glass of wine and light conversation. Once we were relaxed, he looked into my eyes and apologized for his part in our relationship's demise. He shared how much he'd grown and that he'd become an avid reader of spiritual books. I was surprised and relieved. I thanked him for reaching out and healing our connection. We kept in touch and still send each other holiday and birthday greetings.

The following month, I was invited to speak to a local group of reiki healers about meditation and astrology. I looked at my ephemeris and noticed that the moon was back in the sign of Pisces at the time of this lecture. I wanted to keep up the mediumship momentum, so I decided to incorporate spirit messages into my talk. The group wasn't expecting mediumship, so the only pressure on me came from myself.

I meditated at home an hour before the lecture and focused on opening my clairvoyant chakra. When I allowed my third eye to open, I saw spirits. I listened to some of the messages and took a few notes. I figured these spirits belonged to the reiki group, so I urged them to stay around until I arrived at the lecture so I could convey their messages.

I started feeling nervous when I parked my car. I asked for many angels to surround me. I walked into the host's house and saw about twenty-five people in attendance. I shook hands with the host and poured myself a cup of water. I headed for the seat saved for me. After I was formally introduced, I gave a quick summary of my background and elaborated on the importance of dreams. I started to share the profound spirit dream I'd experienced three days after Cashmere died, and suddenly we all heard a loud meow.

Chills ran up and down my spine, and the audience members looked at each other with wide eyes. The owner had a female cat that he had locked in his bedroom during our session, and she had meowed at the precise moment I'd mentioned Cashmere. After learning this, we all shared a great laugh, which seemed to relax and open up everyone for a phenomenal evening. It was another divine, perfect moment.

Next, I spoke about the insight that astrology offers and provided spiritual lessons for each of the twelve zodiac signs. I ended by listing the benefits of meditation, and then I offered to bring through messages from spirits who were present.

Immediately, I saw the spirits that had shown up during my meditation at home. I gave physical descriptions and death conditions, and audience members acknowledged the spirits. I provided very brief messages to four people, concluding with the host, whose mother had passed away three years before. I ended the session by thanking the spirits and saying a closing prayer. I immediately took a bathroom break, and in my solitude, I thanked the angels for coming through for me. I felt euphoric.

When I returned from the bathroom, the room was still silent. Nobody had moved, and many looked stunned. I sat back down and asked if anybody had questions. Some people wanted their dreams analyzed, and others asked psychic-related questions. Many asked for my business cards, and some booked astrological appointments on the spot. After that night, I expanded my astrology readings to include brief mediumship sessions, some numerology, and angel-card readings.

I had only wanted to write self-help, how-to books and resisted writing about my life, but eventually, I adhered to my strong inner guidance to do so, understanding that I had to write a memoir into the narrative. Although I initially found it challenging, especially feeling the emotions attached to the story's painful lessons, after writing it, I felt free from the past and more alive in the present.

Yet writing this book was only one part of the journey. I still had more lessons to learn, especially about self-worth and self-esteem. Much to my chagrin, the literary agents that had initially expressed interest in my book rejected my proposal. I received many rejection letters, one after the other.

I found myself getting more angry and restless, and this affected my writing, especially one day when I received a particularly painful rejection letter. In my initial meeting with this agent, we'd shared a connection. We'd talked about astrology. She was a Pisces, knew her birth chart, and loved the subject. I have a moon in Pisces, and this has always attracted Pisces people to me. I thought we would be a good fit as author and agent. She'd seemed excited about my book, and I'd felt very optimistic. Now, I would have to start my search all over again.

Three hours later I was in my home office still stewing about the rejections. I knew I needed to stop feeling this way, so I immediately went to the gym, ran a few miles on the treadmill, and cleared my mind.

Afterward, I finally realized I had put too much credence on others' approval, especially when it came to my writing. I had invested too much energy trying to be accepted, and I now needed to reclaim my power. A statement echoed in my mind from a Deepak Chopra seminar I'd recently attended: "In order to succeed, you must develop immunity to criticism and to flattery." I had to stop taking the rejections so personally. I had to check in with myself and believe that I was good enough to write, publish, and succeed. Perhaps this was not the right manuscript. I had to believe that the universe had my best interest at heart and would lead me to the right publisher.

I hired a local freelance editor and worked with him for the next few months. In the process, I learned a lot about the wonderful craft of writing. He edited a few of my chapters and assisted me with rewriting a professional query letter and proposal. He also offered a service that included an agent and publisher submission list for my genre. He submitted 150 inquiries through e-mail on my behalf, and still no one was interested.

To stay focused, I next decided to branch out of my region and submit excerpts from my book as inspirational articles for magazines. After all, in order for me to market my book, I needed to expand my media platform nationally. I purchased a few women's magazines that cater to self-help or inspiration. I wasn't a big magazine reader, but I learned that most magazines, for men or women, had inspirational columns and self-help sections. I also purchased the *Writer's Market Deluxe* guide and followed the steps for sending queries to magazine editors.

After many e-mails, cover letters, phone calls, and inquiries, I received no interest. I had never known how tough this new career would be.

I looked back at my working life, which I had begun as a stock boy at a retail store and ended as a senior officer for a major bank. Now I needed to start over in a whole new industry. I wrote metaphysical articles for free, just to get exposure and writing experience. I participated in numerous expos and free public lectures. I also took a media exposure class at a local college for business owners to learn more about TV and radio.

I stepped away from the book drama and vacationed in Santa Fe, New Mexico, for a long weekend with my friend Eli. During my flight, I felt drained and tired and started having body aches. Once we landed, I started sweating and knew I was run down and getting sick. I checked into my hotel, and Eli picked up over-the-counter cold medicine and Tylenol for my fever. I'd just started reading *Archangels and Ascended Masters* by Doreen Virtue and learned that I can call upon certain archangels for specific tasks.

I'd wondered if there was an archangel of health, but I hadn't finish reading the book, and I'd intentionally left it at home with my laptop because I wanted to vacation without interruptions or concentration. I lay in bed praying that I would heal fast. Even though I had a general belief in angels, I didn't know if they had specific names. I yelled, "If there's an archangel of health, please heal me!" I felt delirious with fever and repeated this prayer hundreds of times until I fell asleep.

I woke up the following morning to Eli's knock on the door. He wanted to know if I felt strong enough to go out for breakfast. After a hot shower, I felt well enough, so I ventured out to the plaza and enjoyed a beautiful spring day. The skies were blue and the temperature was in the seventies.

After breakfast, we walked around and enjoyed the architecture of the city. Eli then asked if I felt strong enough to take a ride up to Chimayo, a small city known for a popular church with healing energy. I decided it would be best to go and continue to pray for my full recovery.

The church ceiling was only five feet tall, so I had to duck when I entered. Inside were many pews lined with praying locals and tourists. Statues of every saint ever canonized adorned the walls.

In a back room was a small pit filled with holy dirt. Many lined up to enter and bless themselves. Once Eli and I completed our prayers and blessings, we drove around to see the rest of the city.

Eli spotted a restaurant and asked if we could stop for a light lunch. We were culinary classmates and enjoyed tasting foods from many establishments, so we indulged in a light lunch of soup and salad. Upon exiting the restaurant, Eli noticed a statue of an angel hidden in a shaded corner by the entrance. He said, "Go stand next to that angel statue and I'll snap a picture."

I had been unaware of the statue's presence when I'd entered and would have missed it when I left. I immediately gave Eli my camera and placed my arm around the wing for my photo. After I posed, I looked down by the angel's feet and saw a nameplate that read, "San Raphael Archangel."

"Oh my God," I gasped. Chills ran through me. "I think I've just been led to the archangel of health."

I was still in awe on the drive back to the hotel. I enjoyed the rest of the weekend, and my health recovered quickly. When I arrived home days later, I looked up Archangel Raphael in the angel book and found that he was indeed the archangel of health. I was amazed that my prayers were answered, and I now feel that I'd met a lifelong friend.

Throughout late spring and all of summer, I persevered through challenges. I suffered my first automobile accident and totaled my car—just after paying it off. I found Ashley, my Persian cat, dead in my bedroom one afternoon from an apparent heart attack. I acted as my own PR person, and every time I tried to get on radio and local or cable TV, I was turned down. I also had to evacuate my home and lost power for days on two separate occasions because of hurricanes—all while trying to write this book.

While in my ninth year in a personal cycle, I read my numerology book to see what I needed to do. I was in a period of endings—of tying up loose ends. I looked back and realized that nine years before, I had ended my ties in New York and moved to Florida, and nine years before that, I had left my home and ventured out on my own. At least with some history behind me, I could rely on the testimony of Pythagoras's science of numbers. I was relieved to know that I had to complete my year of endings and that change was on the horizon. I hoped to finally procure a publishing deal.

My persistence started to pay off. While promoting myself and providing astrology sessions at my booth for Tampa's Body, Mind, and Spirit Expo, I received a strong message that confirmed I was on the right path. A gentleman walked by and handed me a flyer. He said, "I have a local talk radio show promoting holistic healing. Would you like to come on my show to discuss astrology?"

I answered, "Absolutely. When would you like to me to appear?" We exchanged contact information, and he contacted me a week later to schedule my appearance.

I had learned from my angel book that Archangel Gabriel is the manager of media and communications. On my way to the studio for my first radio appearance, I asked Archangel Gabriel to assist me in articulating well and coming across as confident. I parked my car, and a parking attendant guided me to a building across the street. I entered but could not find the radio station. I asked a bystander for new directions, but those turned out to be wrong as well. I then asked a third person to guide me, but he didn't know where I was supposed to go. I was lost. I had only five minutes left before airtime. I started to sweat and became anxious.

I went back to the first building and walked around the premises to see if I had missed any hidden entrances or signs promoting the radio station. In the back of the building, I spotted a man about ten feet ahead of me. I immediately recognized him as the host and called out his name. He turned around and led me to the studio. I had two minutes before I went live. I asked Archangel Michael, the manger of strength and protection, to give me courage, and I aced the show. I drove home feeling elated! I thanked the archangels over and over again.

My book was complete and I was in the midst of rewrites. I thoroughly enjoyed the creative process of writing. After the New Year, I attended the second annual writer's conference in San Francisco in hopes of attracting an agent. My trip proved largely fruitless, except for the closing lecture by Jack Canfield, co-author of the *Chicken Soup for the Soul* series.

Jack provided many pieces of inspiration, including stories about his persistence, which eventually paid off. He said that before the first *Chicken Soup* book was published, he was rejected over one hundred times. He felt that all the rejection was the universe's way of testing how much he really wanted to be published. He inspired us to never give up on our dreams.

His testimony sealed my belief in myself. Whether this book would be self-published or traditionally published, I determined that it would be published. However, it would be done in divine time, not mine. After spending thousands of dollars on writers' conferences, supplies, and writing services, including a freelance editor, I surrendered the outcome to the universe. I asked that I be guided me to the right publishing deal and be kept aware of any signs that would show me how and when my work of love would be published.

I recalled a statement from *Many Lives, Many Masters,* by Brian L. Weiss, MD, a profound message from one of the masters: "Patience and timing … everything comes when it must come. A life cannot be rushed, cannot be worked on a schedule as so many people want it to be." I now felt it wasn't the right time, so I put the manuscript away.

Patience and discipline are important lessons scripted in my astrology chart. Part of me thought I must have been insane to script such a tough life this time around. I must have decided that if I needed to come back to this planet, I would really make it worth my while. So in addition to intimacy, abandonment, and self-esteem issues, I'd thrown in issues of patience and discipline for good measure. Although I viewed challenges and obstacles as spiritual lessons, doing so wasn't easy. I found these lessons frustrating.

The following week, I received an invitation to attend Eli's niece's wedding in Delhi, India. Eli had often invited me to his country to meet his family and tour the historic sites, but my vacation schedule had never allowed me. Now that I had ample time, I wanted to get away from the entire publishing saga, so I gladly accepted. I booked my flight and wondered what ancient India would show and teach me.

CHAPTER TWELVE

INDIA

It was one in the morning local time when my nonstop thirteen-hour flight landed. It took almost an hour to go through customs and immigration and another hour to reclaim my bags.

After exchanging some US dollars for Indian rupees, I wheeled my belongings up the long passageway to the visitor area, where I faced a bizarre scene. There must have been over a thousand people lined up on either side of the walkway calling out names, trying to claim those arriving. I stopped and put on my glasses so I could see where my mini entourage waited for me. I soon spotted Eli and his friends flailing their arms to get my attention. I was elated to finally see a familiar face. I hugged everyone, relieved to have arrived safely.

A few miles from the airport, the cloud of pollution finally lifted, and I was able to see my surroundings more clearly. I noticed that stop signs and red lights were only suggestions, not signals that had to be obeyed. The other visitors had generously invited me to sit in the front of the cab, clearly knowing how chaotic and adventurous the long forty-five minute ride to the hotel would be. They had experienced the same frightening cab ride a day earlier upon their arrival. I closed my eyes and breathed deeply every time I saw the cab edge by other vehicles. I couldn't believe how heavy the traffic was in the middle of the night. It made New York City seem empty by comparison. Once I arrived in my hotel room, I feel fast asleep.

We spent the first couple of days in Delhi touring temples, mosques, and tombs. We also shopped at the big Kaan market downtown. The shopping area was so large that it took us three days to visit all the stores.

I especially enjoyed old Delhi, which really gave me a sense of classic India. The city was so crowded that people literally rubbed elbows on the street. The many shops were narrow, small, and sandwiched between dark alleys on every block. The garment district was flourishing, with both locals and tourists purchasing goods.

Our next voyage was a five-hour trip to Agra to visit one of the Wonders of the World, the Taj Mahal. We boarded the rental van at six in the morning while the sky was still dark. When the morning dusk arrived, I was captivated by what I saw.

The infrastructure was almost nonexistent. Once we left Delhi, the streets were mostly dirt roads. We drove through many villages where animals roamed the streets. I counted twelve species of animals during our trip, including monkeys, cows, goats, pigs, cats, dogs, camels, horses, and a black bear.

The overpopulated villages were dirty and poor. Many families had only a bike as their sole mode of transportation. Many women held infants in their arms while riding sidesaddle on the backs of bicycles while their husbands pedaled standing up. The homes were made of old aluminum, and many had graffiti sprayed on them. The dirt roads were so small that the van had to constantly swerve to avoid bystanders and bikers. Our driver nearly missed a senior man walking with a cane. At the last moment, the elderly gentleman tossed his cane and jump-skipped to avoid being hit.

The bumpy roads gave me motion sickness. I prayed that I wouldn't get sick in the middle of nowhere. I didn't want to sour the voyage for the other eight passengers, who were just as traumatized by the poor living conditions.

We stopped halfway for a quick breakfast in a remote restaurant with only a few people inside. It was a refreshing break from the mobs of people we'd come to expect.

We finally arrived in Agra. Once we passed security and entered the gates, the Taj Mahal was majestic. The grand entrance to the grounds that led up to main building was beautiful, the terra cotta and white archway were engraved with passages from the Koran. The covered entrance opened up to the gardens at the feet of the beautiful white castle.

Taj Mahal means "Castle of Love," and it definitely lived up to its billing. The long walkway to the fountain, where the late Princess Diana and ex-President Bill Clinton took their photos while sitting on the white bench, was filled with many slim, manicured trees, regal in their own way, almost mocking the castle behind.

At the foot of the building, we were instructed to remove our shoes. Before I entered the castle, I looked up the side of the building, in awe of the symmetry. I'd heard a tour guide mention that every stone had been laid precisely to accommodate the emperor shah's wishes. The white marble shimmered in the evening, reflecting an orange glow during a full moon. The emperor had the castle built in the 1600s to honor his late wife, Queen Arjumand Bano Begum, who'd died while giving birth to their fourteenth child.

Once inside, we couldn't take any more photos, because the queen's body was enshrined in the crypt. The tour guide said that it had taken seventeen years to complete the building and that every worker who had laid a brick had had his thumb cut off to deter any temptation to replicate the castle. The emperor had been deeply stricken by grief, and he'd channeled his pain by making sure the castle was built perfectly, one stone at a time. Once the palace was complete, the emperor's eldest son had him jailed and then killed the rest of his brothers to wrest the throne from his father.

Single arched towers on either side flanked the castle. They had been engineered to fall away if an earthquake ever hit. Behind was the river Jamuna, a holy body of water running east. Many prayed by the water for healing.

After our visit, we ate a delicious lunch at a local restaurant and then headed back to Delhi. On the ride back, I chatted with a native about religion. I'd learned that the country's three main religions were Hinduism, Islam, and Sikhism. Although other religions, including Christianity, were practiced there, we discussed the three main ones.

I'd learned that Hindus prayed to different gods and goddesses depending on the specific request, similar to the way Catholics prayed to the saints.

One god that many Hindus prayed to was Ganesh, the remover of obstacles. I'd heard of Ganesh years before, and I'd invoked his presence and power during my writing rituals. I'd only known then that he was the Hindu god to invoke before any ritual and that his elephant head mystified me. The native explained that in Indian mythology, Ganesh's father, Shiva, argued with his wife, Parvati, and in his haste, chopped off the head of Ganesh. In her grief, Parvati impulsively chopped off the head of the nearest animal, which happened to be a baby elephant, and placed it on her son so he could have a head again.

I was intrigued by this religious figure. I'd seen so many pictures of him. I always kept a pad and pen in my knapsack, and I took them out and asked Eli if he could educate me further about Ganesh.

He said, "Ganesh is the youngest son of Shiva and Parvati. He's a prankster and loves to eat sweets, especially ledoos, the yellow balls of sugar. He has a big belly. He's the god that removes obstacles; essentially, he's the god of new beginnings and prosperity. He's also the favorite god in the state of Maharashtra, in Bombay. They celebrate him in many ways, including by praying to Ganesh idols. Individual homes have small statues of him, and the community has a big one."

"He is really beloved," I remarked.

I also learned that at the Ganesh festival held in September before Diwali, the festival of lights, the neighbors bring out the small Ganesh idols and dance their way from their residences. They prop up the big

Ganesh on a truck as a float and gather around it as it heads to the beach. Children dressed in cordas sing and dancing throughout the celebration. Some even walk ten miles or more.

"Sounds like a huge event," I said.

The native continued, "When the float arrives at the shore, the men then carry the large Ganesh on planks over their shoulders. They march to the beat of drums and head into the water until they are completely submerged. There are many people coming from every direction holding up their big Ganeshes in pride and honor. There's much fanfare and jubilation."

"Tell me more," I begged.

I learned that Ganesh is also mischievous and clever. To illustrate this, the local told a story that described how he handled a special request from his father. Shiva told Ganesh and his two older brothers to circle the universe seven times and then come back. The older two sons circled the universe. Ganesh circled his parents.

Shiva said, "What are you doing? I told you to circle the universe."

Ganesh replied, "I did. My mother and father are my universe."

I was moved by this story. "Boy, he is clever." I smiled.

The sun was setting, and the dimly lit road became difficult to travel. There were many bicycles on the road, and many of them were missing reflectors, and I feared for their safety. I closed my eyes to prevent further anxiety and focused on how calm and soothed I'd feel after a long, hot shower. That helped me get through the five-hour ride back.

Eli had surprised me by purchasing silk so I could have a custom-made suit jacket called a *jodhpuri*, a traditional garment worn at formal affairs, for his niece's wedding. I spent the better part of the following afternoon being fitted for my new garment.

The wedding celebration lasted the entire weekend. The day before the event, the groom's parents hosted an afternoon gathering in an outdoor courtyard. The weather was fantastic, sunny and warm. The dress code was casual. As we entered the luncheon, we were initiated with a *bindi*, a red dot placed in the center of the forehead symbolizing the third eye. After the beautiful luncheon, we headed back to the hotel to rest up for the evening gathering.

The evening attire was formal. The bride's father hosted a dinner on military grounds, a perk he'd earned from his thirty-year allegiance to the Indian military. The food was delicious, further feeding my appetite for Indian cuisine. I'd always enjoyed worldly cuisine, but the Indian flavors and spices really opened my palate.

After dinner, many lined up to get their hands painted with henna (another Indian tradition in which symbols are hand painted from the fingers up to the elbows). Traditionally, the bride and her wedding party have it done, and it's optional for the rest of the wedding attendees. Once all the ladies were painted, I saw some men get in line. I joined them and had the *om*, the Buddhist symbol for God, painted on the center of my right palm. I had someone snap a photo of it with my camera and then walked around with an open palm to let the paint dry. It looked awesome, and I felt a strong connection to the wedding's energy.

The next evening was the big event. Those of us who were leaving the next day decided to go shopping one last time in the afternoon. I bought souvenirs for friends and family and looked for a hand-painted sculpture of Ganesh for my home. Upon viewing the many Ganesh statues, Eli, who had accompanied us, told me to look into the eyes of each sculpture and choose the one with happy and peaceful eyes.

After a few minutes, I picked a wooden sculpture painted in red, green, and brown. The eyes were so beautiful, they could easily have been mistaken for the eyes of a goddess. It reminded me of my belief that everyone has both male and female energy within.

The wedding took place outdoors. The weather was a cool fifty degrees Fahrenheit. January had been chosen for the wedding because the cool weather was auspicious for a long union, as was the date (22), a master number in numerology that ensured power and longevity.

Our van brought us to the entrance, and plush red carpets led us to the beautiful and spacious outdoor courtyard. The manicured landscape was dotted with tents decorated in white lights. Off to the left was a band dressed in white. The tents where the bride and groom exchanged their vows were both dressed in red, a color believed to ward off evil and negative energy, and gold. The seating area to the right was draped in red chiffon tied with huge white bows. The food stations surrounding the grounds were simmered with many classic Indian dishes from soups to desserts. The aroma was intoxicating.

The crowd gathered to await the soon-to-be-united couple. The bride and groom kept themselves shielded from each other before the wedding, just as couples in the Western world traditionally do.

The bride arrived first. Her immediate family members surrounded her. She looked beautiful in a maroon silk gown with many accessories, including a crystal pendant dangling on her forehead. Ornate dress was auspicious for Indian brides, I learned. She waived at us before being whisked away to a private room to pray before the event.

The groom arrived shortly thereafter wearing a burgundy corda and a red hat called a *sherwani*. He was jovial and proud. His family members, including his sister, mom, and dad, flanked him.

Since the bride and groom were from two different states, two officiants presided over the ceremonies, one for each state.

The groom's ceremony took place first. The bride was guided up onto a platform and stood at one end. A white sheet separated her from her soon-to-be husband. Parents from both sides also stood on the platform in support of their children's matrimony.

The groom's ceremony lasted about thirty minutes. The couple exchanged mantras and many statements through the veil while the hundreds of attendees watched. Once the couple had completed their vows, the sheet was dropped and their eyes met. It was a magical moment. The couple joined hands, and we all clapped in jubilation.

After the groom's ceremony, the couple bowed and kissed the feet of every elder attendee in a ritual of respect and longevity for their union. Once this ceremony ended, we walked to the other end of the grounds to partake in the bride's ceremony.

This ceremony started out very differently. Guests sat surrounding the couple, instead of standing like we had for the groom's ceremony.

The bride sat next to her groom with their respective families behind them. A roaring fire separated the other officant and the couple.

This ceremony lasted forty-five minutes, with the couple exchanging many vows and prayers. Once they were pronounced husband and wife, they stood facing the officiant, and then the groom took the bride's hands and led her around the roaring fire seven times, a common ritual in traditional Indian weddings called *satpadi*. When they had finished, everyone clapped and congratulated the couple.

That evening after packing my suitcase, I sat up in bed and thought about my trip. I'd learned so many things about India. Besides a greater understanding of its culture, rituals, and tourist and religious sites, I'd learned that citizens respected each other. In a city of seventeen million, I never saw one act of unkindness or rudeness. The beggars and street peddlers were no more aggressive or desperate than those in other countries.

The only weapon I'd seen was at the Taj Mahal: a security guard had a rifle in a holder. I'm sure a city with so many people does have crime and violence, but on the whole, I felt safe and never threatened. While many shops competed for tourist money, merchants had an understanding that everyone must get along and respect each other.

I was extremely appreciative for the opportunity to travel so far and to witness another part of this amazing planet. The experience made me more grateful for my existence and for the luxuries I had back home. I felt more alive by living in the moment. This trip prepared me for the amazing opportunities that surfaced almost immediately after I arrived home.

CHAPTER THIRTEEN

LESSONS

Soon after returning from India, I received a phone call from a gentleman who led a nonprofit organization for lesbian, gays, bisexual, transgender, and straight teens in high school. The organization promoted tolerance and unity among all teens in the county. He asked if I would volunteer my time to provide the teens with astrology sessions at the organization's fundraiser.

I immediately felt good about doing it. I knew I could make a difference in these teens' lives if I gave them inspirational guidance and educated them about overcoming challenges and obstacles. I knew how difficult teen life could be, and I wanted to give them optimism for adulthood. I agreed to volunteer my services, and the event was a hit.

A week later during an outdoor festival, I saw another volunteer from the teen event. He introduced me to a man named Fred who hosted a weekly show on local cable TV. When Fred found out I was an astrologer, he immediately asked if I would be a guest on his show. I gladly accepted, and we exchanged business cards.

Within two weeks, Fred e-mailed me to book me for a live one-hour call-in show. I had taken a course on media exposure a year before, but learning something in a classroom was very different from experiencing it. I was both nervous and excited to make my TV debut. I searched the Internet for more tips on TV appearances. Then I heard my inner voice say, "All you need to do is focus on your actions and words." I then realized that I had no control over the production of the show, including what happened in the control room, so I began to relax and gain more confidence.

On the day of my TV debut, I napped peacefully in the afternoon. Before I left for the studio, I summoned the assistance of Archangels Gabriel and Michael.

When I arrived at the studio, the host gave me a tour of the station, including set and the control room. I looked through the glass partition and saw a crew setting up. It felt surreal.

I waited in the green room until I was called. When it was my turn to come on, I stepped onto the raised set and took a seat behind a long glass coffee table. One of the stage crew miked me and tested my audio. I looked around and greeted the three cameramen and stage manager. Once everything was tested, a deep silence took over. I heard the stage manager say, "Ten seconds." My heart raced. I sat up straight, took a deep breath, and saw the red light go on over the center camera.

The host interviewed me, and then we took at least fifteen calls. I enjoyed doing live, on-the-spot astrology consultations using my ephemeris as a planetary guide. The show was a success. Those who had been in the control room came onto the set after the show and congratulated me. It was another euphoric experience.

At this point, I focused on astrology sessions and was no longer doing the short mediumship sessions since I didn't feel strongly called to mediumship.

A week later, to keep up the media momentum, I e-mailed a local reporter who wrote a weekly column in a liberal and progressive paper about new and exciting people and businesses in the neighborhood.

I offered the reporter a free astrological consultation in exchange for some written exposure.

A week later, to my delight, a senior editor replied, "I found your website very interesting." She assigned a reporter and a photographer to come to my home office two weeks later.

On that big day, I sat nervously awaiting the reporter and photographer. I had scanned every inch of my home and office to make sure everything was neat and professional. When the reporter, a very attractive blonde woman, showed up exactly on time, I welcomed her in with a sturdy handshake and my customary big smile.

As I did with all my clients, I offered her bottled water and allowed her to get comfortable. She told me that she secretly thought the other reporters were envious that she had been assigned to me. It seemed that many in her office had a keen interest in astrology. She made it clear that she could not accept a free consultation from me, because doing so conflicted with her company policy. She then pulled out a legal pad and tape recorder. I did the same. I had learned in my media class to also record everything I said so I wouldn't be misquoted in print. She asked many questions about my personal development and what had led me to become an astrologer.

Then the photographer arrived. He was a large burly man with a crushing handshake. He rejected my request for water and asked where I wanted to have my photo taken. While I sat down and continued to answer the reporter's questions, the photographer snapped away in silence.

Once the pictures were taken, the photographer shook my hand and immediately left to shoot another assignment. The reporter sat comfortably for three more hours, and we enjoyed a meaningful discussion on astrology and spirituality. She even asked to speak with Alexis for further details.

Two weeks later I picked up ten copies of the newspaper and was overjoyed by what I read. The reporter depicted me as an astrological life coach and advisor who empowered those who sought my services. The color photos tastefully accentuated the article. I went out dancing with friends that night to celebrate.

The cable TV show contacted me again, and I became a regular monthly guest. In fact, I was given the chance to host my own segment of the show providing a monthly astrological forecast. It was exhilarating to be a host, just me and the camera. I had known after my first TV appearance that I was on the right track, so I enjoyed myself and developed more faith.

One of my close friends, a talented musician named Trevor who had also moved to Florida from New York years before, was also on the spiritual path, and we often discussed numerology, astrology, and angel encounters. We also talked about our family karma and our mutual lesson to have faith that we would achieve our career success. We supported each other and had a natural connection. Every time I attended his performances, he dedicated Billy Joel's "New York State of Mind" to me.

I increasingly spent more time with friends like Trevor. I enjoyed building friendships with people I could be silly with and also have meaningful spiritual conversations with. I stopped hanging out with those who judged, criticized, and gossiped. I had to learn lessons in boundaries, so whenever I felt drained around certain people, I choose to step back and save my energy. My work as a healer, helper, and counselor was an expression of love, and I needed to respect my energy. I learned that compassion, sensitivity, and support fulfilled me, and I no longer felt like a pushover or doormat.

The following week I had vivid dreams, and one in particular felt like a strong promotion. A spirit told me to contact my friend Judy in New York and tell her to heal her relationship with her father. I got the impression that he was going to cross over to the other side within the year. Toward the end of the dream, Judy's younger brother was deeply upset about this, and then I woke.

I thought about the message, and it felt real to me. I hadn't been given any details about the possibility of his transition, but I'd made an agreement to help those on earth with messages from the other side, so I e-mailed Judy that morning, wording the message carefully so I wouldn't alarm her.

She replied later that morning and said she didn't know what to think. I responded that sometimes my dreams didn't come true but that I had to give whatever messages I received. Judy had a great sense of humor, and we had always cracked each other up, so in typical fashion, she replied, "Thanks for the warning. You are now relieved of your karmic obligation—you freak!"

In the meantime, Andrew, a neighbor of a friend in California, e-mailed me to say he'd be attending a conference in Tampa and wanted to meet me for dinner. We'd met briefly during my last trip to California and had a nice spiritual connection.

Andrew arrived the following week. During supper, we talked about our career aspirations. Although he had known I was an astrologer, he was surprised to hear that I was also a writer and speaker. When I told him that I'd just finished a manuscript and wanted it to be published by Hay House, he looked pensive. He asked if the founder of that publishing house was Louise Hay.

I said yes, and to my surprise, he told me that his friend Tom in San Diego was acquainted with Louise Hay. He offered to contact Tom to connect me with Louise or someone at Hay House.

A few days later Andrew sent an e-mail addressed to me and copied Tom. I immediately e-mailed Tom to introduce myself. Tom replied the next day offering to help. In exchange, I offered Tom a free review of his astrological chart. He was receptive to my offer, and we became acquaintances.

I was so grateful that my connection to the universe was growing stronger. Every moment of every day, I chose to enjoy my life, or at least to be fully present.

On my thirty-eighth birthday, I received an e-mail from Tom saying that he'd referred me to a gentleman named Don who personally knew Louise and could offer me insight into connecting with her. I immediately e-mailed my new contact and offered him a free astrological consultation in exchange for his assistance. I patiently waited for his reply.

Later that day, I had plans to go swimming with the dolphins with Becky, my new spiritual buddy. Since dolphins have healing abilities,

I wanted to ask them to open and heal my heart so I could attract a spiritual mate into my life.

On my special day, Becky and I entered the chilly waters with the precious dolphins. With each step, the water got deeper, and the dolphins got closer. I silently asked, *Please tell me what I need to learn from the dolphins.*

After kissing and tickling the dolphins for over half an hour, enjoying every minute, the lesson bestowed upon me was clear: I needed to have more *fun.*

In doing so, I would also learn another lesson: faith. Although I desired a dream house, a sexy and spiritual partner, many published books, and financial abundance, I didn't have to think or worry about that all the time. I could declare my desires, hopes, and wishes and work toward them, but I could have fun along the way and leave everything else to the universe. I kept my promise that I wouldn't spend another dime to be published until the universe gave me a clear and open path to follow.

Instead I invested my money in building my media platform. I signed in a three-month contract with a popular Internet radio station called Voice America based in Seattle, Washington. This package included a radio commercial, advertisement on the website, and three live interviews. I wanted to expand my astrology business to the West Coast.

I also placed an ad in a national publication called *Radio-TV Interview Report* (RTIR), which is distributed to radio and TV stations across the country. I received a lot of invitations and did a lot of radio shows that year.

During the summer of 2006, I again lectured at the American Federation of Astrologers convention. This year's event was held in Louisville, Kentucky. I really enjoyed public speaking, but more importantly, I was educating others.

During dinner one night, I mentioned to Trevor that Louise Hay was turning eighty soon and that I would have loved to be invited to her party as a guest of Tom's or Dan's but felt uncomfortable asking them. After all, I hadn't met Tom or Dan and didn't know their marital status. In fact, I hadn't heard from Dan in almost a month, and he hadn't replied to an e-mail I'd sent several weeks before.

During a full-moon lunar eclipse one evening, I heard from Dan in California. We had a pleasant phone conversation. As the conversation wound down, he asked me if I wanted to attend Louise's eightieth birthday party in three weeks. I immediately accepted. Dan and I were mentally on the same page. I started to mention that I'd like to give Louise a free astrology session as a birthday gift, and Dan suggested it at the same time. He contacted Louise's secretary for Louise's birth information and e-mailed it to me later that day.

My vision of attending her birthday party was coming true. My thoughts and actions were manifesting my desires. I called Trevor to share the news, and he was elated for me.

I booked my flight, hotel, and rental car the next day and started to tweak my manuscript for what seemed like the hundredth time. I spent many hours over two nights delineating Louise's chart. I wanted to give her a decade-by-decade synopsis of her eighty years on earth. I wanted to do the best job I'd ever done.

I also updated my website to include excerpts from my book and links to my recent media appearances, including some national radio shows. I packed my business cards for any possible networking opportunities. If this was the divine door opening, I wanted to make sure I could run through it. I didn't know what to expect at the party, but I knew it would be magical just to meet Louise, not to mention the high probability that I'd meet many literary personnel, including some of my favorite Hay House authors.

I flew to California and met Dan at his home. He welcomed me with a hug and gave me a tour of the house. He was also a lover of cats and showed me the kitten he'd recently adopted. After a brief conversation, we drove to the birthday gala together. We barely entered the lobby of the ballroom at the Four Seasons when Dan said, "There's Louise." I turned around, and there she stood, five feet from me. Dan hugged her, wished her a happy birthday, and introduced me to her. I shook her hand, and Dan immediately had us pose for a photo. *Wow, what an opening to a party!* I thought. *This is going to be fun.*

The ballroom was dimly lit and the party in full swing. Hundreds of people were enjoying the atmosphere. After an hour of mingling, Dan and I decided to sample some of the delicious food. I grabbed a plate and wandered to one of the many food sections. I handed my plate to a server. While he scooped a spoonful of vegetables onto my plate, I looked to my right and saw Doreen Virtue standing beside me. Surprised, I said, "Hi, Doreen. It's great to see you." She said, "It's great to see you again."

I must have left a strong impression on her during the three-day mediumship course. She always recognized me during her book signings at her yearly "I Can Do It" conferences in Tampa, Florida. After we exchanged greetings, Dan and I sat to eat dinner.

The rest of the evening was awesome. I bumped into Louise twice and had meaningful discussions with her. Dan told her I was an astrologer and that I had recorded an astrology session as a birthday gift. She seemed intrigued and looked forward to hearing the CD.

We left around midnight. I dropped Dan at home and finally made it back to the hotel. I called Trevor and shared my memories from the party and my hope to be part of the Hay House family one day.

I had plans the following evening to have dinner with Dan and Tom. On my way to the restaurant, Alexis called me and said, "Judy's father died today in a car accident." I was shocked. The premonition I'd received a few months earlier had come true. I shared my premonition dream with Alexis, and she was also shocked. I had hoped Judy had mended her relationship with her father. I rushed Alexis off the phone because I wanted to speak with Judy. Unfortunately I was unable to reach her, so I left her a compassionate voice mail and drove to the restaurant in a fog.

I flew home the next day thinking about Judy and her family. She hadn't returned my call, but I decided to fly to New Jersey for the funeral. Once I landed in Tampa, I powered on my cell phone and found one voice mail from Dan. He said that Louise had contacted him to say that her birth time and location had been incorrect on the astrology chart. He pleaded that I call him as soon as possible.

I couldn't believe it. I was so tired from the long flight, and now I was angry! All the time and effort I'd spent creating this memorable gift had been for naught. I grew angrier each minute as the plane taxied to the gate.

Once I deplaned, I called Dan back. He apologized for giving me the wrong birth information and sensed that I was unhappy. He immediately put things in a positive perspective by saying, "Louise called me today and wanted me to give you her phone number so you can call her. She feels bad that you were given the wrong birth information. But now you have a chance to speak with her directly and to possibly build a friendship."

I now looked at this mishap as an opportunity. When I checked my e-mails later that evening, I found one from Louise containing her correct birth information, her phone number, and a request that I contact her directly. Since it was too late to call, I sent an e-mail reply and executed the correct chart within days. I asked her to confirm receipt of the updated chart when she had time.

Within the week, Louise not only confirmed receipt of the corrected session, but she also wrote, "I have just finished both your astrological readings for me and I am so pleased. They are the best readings I have ever had. Thank you very much."

I was beyond elated. I called Dan to share the news. He said, "This is now your chance to get published. Send her your manuscript to read." But I felt uneasy asking her. I'd just establish a rapport as astrologer and client. I barely knew her and felt that asking her for a huge favor was inappropriate.

I thanked Dan again for introducing me to Louise. After we hung up, I replied to Louise thanking her for the testimony.

It was now fall of 2006. Aunt Nancy's husband, Richard, had struggled with Parkinson's and cancer, and he finally left his body in November. At his wake in New Jersey, a priest from Aunt Nancy's Catholic church said a prayer at the funeral home. Alexis and I met with Father Jerome afterward since we needed to obtain a copy of the scriptures we would read at the funeral the next day. After he briefed us, Alexis stepped away, and I had a private conversation with him.

I asked, "Father, have you ever dreamt of or felt the spirit of a departed loved one?"

He looked into my eyes and said, "Son, I not only feel them... I see them."

"Really?" I replied. I'd been so removed from church that I hadn't known how he'd react, and I definitely didn't expect a priest to admit he was clairvoyant.

Father Jerome continued, "Soon after my mother and sister passed away, I saw them visit me in my bedroom. I was so touched by their presence. It gave me a lot of comfort. I now keep a picture of my mom, sister, and the Virgin Mary on my bedside table."

I shared stories of some of my visits from my own departed loved ones, and we had a wonderful connection. We then shook hands and said we'd see each other tomorrow at the church. I flew back to Florida the day after the funeral.

After the holidays ended, I looked forward to 2007, but the real estate market started to collapse, and so did the economy. My book hadn't been published, and my astrology business slowed substantially. My media appearances were sporadic. My savings were diminishing. I felt forced to go back to corporate America and felt dejected, saddened, and angry.

I updated my resume and contacted my prior employer but couldn't land a job. I applied for many other jobs in different industries, trying to keep my options open, but wasn't contacted for an interview. I was shocked by how difficult it was to find employment. I felt I was an ideal candidate for many jobs. I'd been steadily employed for more than twenty years, had worked for major organizations, was fairly well educated, and had no arrest record or other legal issues. I was dumbfounded and extremely frustrated. I became desperate and enraged about my circumstances. I prayed but still felt powerless.

After six long months, I finally landed a temporary job but was laid off after New Year's. I hadn't worked long enough at the temp position to be eligible for unemployment benefits. Again I couldn't find employment and started to fall behind on bills. I relied on whatever astrology money I generated to eat and feed the cats I had adopted the year before. I became furious with the universe!

Aunt Nancy had recently relocated to Florida to start a new chapter, and she assisted me during my difficult times. I reached out to friends, who networked hard for me. Months passed, and I was now in a dire situation. My mortgage had fallen behind, and my anxiety was through the roof. A friend I'd become close to in recent years suggested I file for bankruptcy. I hadn't even thought that was an option. It had never entered my mind. I had planned to go on hardship programs available for my credit card debt, but now that wasn't an option. The equity on my home evaporated, and I had no other resources to borrow from. Unemployed and stressed out, I took my friend's advice and filed for bankruptcy. I had to sell my car to pay the attorney and pay up the mortgage since I didn't want to lose my home. Aunt Nancy supported my only choice and offered to take me food shopping and lend me her car if I were called for an interview.

The day I sold my car and officially filed bankruptcy was a tough day. I felt depressed and lost. I truly understood why people felt trapped and committed suicide. Although running away or ending my life did cross my mind, I never attempted or even seriously considered these actions. I hit bottom. I drank beer and chain-smoked cigarettes (a bad habit I had broken many years before) until I was numb.

Day after day, I sat behind my computer and applied for hundreds of jobs. I had grown more detached from my domicile and applied in other cities and states, as I was willing to relocate. Soon, I didn't care where I lived as long as I could earn a living and have my pets. They were my first priority.

After a few weeks, I was finally contacted for an interview for a sales position with a bank. The location was only a few miles from home. I borrowed Aunt Nancy's car and determined to stay calm and detached but confident throughout the interview. Within an hour, I was offered the job pending a drug test. The very next morning, I took and passed the drug test, and within a week, I had a start date for my orientation. The salary was low, but something was better than nothing. I had a job.

I reached out to friends for assistance with transportation. Within a few weeks, I was able to afford a very cheap car with high mileage. It didn't have air-conditioning, but it ran pretty well for the commute. Once my bankruptcy was discharged, I was able to breathe a little easier. I could finally afford air-conditioning in my car, but it would take some time to recover from this financial mess.

Slowly but surely, I felt the enormity of what I had survived. Numerous times I replayed everything I'd experienced in the few years since my career leap, and I became angry when I thought of the huge financial risk I had taken. I battled myself for a long time. It took me many years to stop the inner judgment and criticism and find peace.

I needed to forgive myself, but I also needed to know why everything had happened. Had I been too idealistic and not realistic enough? Had I misinterpreted all the signs? Did I have an unconscious fear of success? Did I really believe in myself, or was I following a dead-end dream? I went through scenario after scenario. I needed to break down and process my life to understand what I had misunderstood and what lessons I needed to learn.

When I had embarked on my publishing journey, I'd meditated each morning, envisioning having my book published by Hay House and its worldwide success. My focused intent had not brought about the desired result, but it had attracted Louise Hay into my life as a client. She'd commissioned me to provide yearly astrological updates and had also recommended me to others. When I thought about what she symbolized to me, the words *healer* and *entrepreneur* came to me. She had started her own publishing company after she couldn't get published. I figured that's what I need to do. Since I'd decided not to spend another dime going the traditional publishing route, I would learn to self-publish when I could afford it.

Now, I needed divine assistance, but I had a major block from trusting it. How could I have received numerous clear signs to make a career change only to wind up more frustrated and confused?

I couldn't answer that question, so I detached from all my dreams and focused on my new job. I also balanced my life by dating again.

One day, while reading *The Law of Attraction* by Esther and Jerry Hicks, I had an epiphany. The book said that emotions are the magnet of manifestation. If you are sad, angry, and depressed, especially for a long period of time, you will attract negative experiences, since the emotions you're feeling are negative. What a huge revelation. I realized that I'd felt confused, misled, rejected, frustrated, and angry for a while and so had attracted my financial collapse. I knew I believed in myself since I had taken the risk to grow and expand, to fulfill my spiritual mission, but I hadn't been aware of how my more deep-seated emotions could manifest consequences. Unconsciously, I had taken loss and rejection too personally, and I paid a price. This was a great insight, since suffering is neither noble nor the universe's plan for us.

I also learned that the age of thirty-nine had many karmic implications in astrology because of a Neptune transit. I was laid off, went through bankruptcy, and subsequently got hired for a new job, all at age thirty-nine. With the knowledge of my emotions and Neptune, I started to feel less victimized and more empowered.

I wrote a list of what I'd learned from the last few years and read it often. I wanted to make sure I learned these lessons so I could feel more peace. My list read:

1) Do not feel bad for too long or you will attract a negative situation or experience.
2) Continue to believe in yourself. You are a truthful person with a message to help others.
3) If I can think it and *feel* it, I can attract and manifest it.
4) Remember to have fun and get enough rest while working on any project.
5) Never accept no for an answer, and never give up!

6) Rejection or criticism is merely someone else's opinion, not mine.
7) Correct mistakes with positive reinforcement, not punishment.
8) Do not attack, overreact, or become defensive.
9) Have patience and faith, and persevere.

I continued to feed my mind with spiritual literature to keep me positive. Many years before, I'd purchased a book called *A Course in Miracles* by the Foundation for Inner Peace. I finally picked it up off the shelf and became engrossed in its contents. It is an extremely thought-provoking book filled with Jesus's teachings, wisdom, and truth.

The lessons are communicated in the most effective and loving tone I'd ever read. The lessons easily penetrated my essence, and every time I read its messages, I felt intoxicated.

One of the many revelations I encountered was the message of the crucifixion. When I initially encountered this chapter, I closed the book and took a break. I'd had a jaded opinion of the crucifixion from my Catholic upbringing. I recalled many church personnel saying, "Jesus died for our sins." It was a teaching that implied guilt, and it didn't sit right with me. I'd never felt close to Jesus and didn't really understand the crucifixion.

When I eventually read this section, I was amazed to learn its main messages: First, harming the body doesn't harm the soul. You can never harm something that is real and indestructible, and energy doesn't die. The body is not the true self; the soul is. Second, anger and violence are a by-products of the ego, that false part of us that is destructive. The true self is here to create, to enlighten, to heal, and to *love*! Judgment, criticism, hatred, anger, and violence are all behaviors of ego. Third, and most important, we must forgive. Now that I had healed my misperception, I felt more connected to Jesus's teachings.

I also learned that rejection is never real, because all people are made from the same divine imprint of love. So our spiritual DNA is part of, not separate from, the universe, or God. I became more aware—I saw more readily how people, places, and things were motivated by either love or fear (ego). I thanked the universe for leading me to this wondrous book and its valuable lessons in the landscape of knowledge.

I settled into my new work routine. During my afternoon break one day, I received a voice mail advising me that my friend Evelyn had suddenly passed away from an apparent heart attack.

I initially took the news calmly, but as the day wore on, I became sad and gloomy. Evelyn and I had been friends for almost twenty years. Although our friendship had faded in the last two years, it was hard to erase the memories of the past. I especially recalled our memorable trip back from Cassadaga when we listened to her psychic reading and heard the voice of her deceased mother. I knew she was now reunited with her family, including her brother, who had died the year before. I attended her wake and reconnected with her family and friends.

The next evening, I joined a couple of her close friends for dinner. While discussing a memory with everyone, I suddenly felt a tug on my suit jacket. This startled me and stopped me in midsentence. I just stared at the bottom of my jacket and was amazed. I then shared what happened, and everyone else was amazed. We acknowledged Evelyn's presence and had a great laugh. We continued to honor her life by sharing more memories.

CHAPTER FOURTEEN

ACCEPTANCE

My full-time job, work as an animal activist, and my astrology business made the next few years fly by. My neighbor and I fixed the many stray cats in the community by using the Humane Society's trap-and-release program. Once the feral cats were spayed or neutered and vaccinated, I housed them overnight in my spare room and released them the next day. We also found an organization that fostered and adopted the kittens.

Although I was grateful to have steady employment and income, my life had not been flowing for years. Despite interviewing for many higher paying jobs, every time I tried to better my financial situation, something didn't allow me to get hired. Interview after interview went great, but the jobs were eventually offered to others.

Part of me knew I was not at peace working for corporate America, that I wasn't offered the jobs because my heart wasn't in it. I was in a funk and needed to change my life.

I rejoined a gym and started working out again. My body had carried too much negativity in recent years from drinking, smoking, and sowing my oats. I was diminishing my light. I needed to release toxins and take better care of myself. I espoused to start a new and healthy chapter in my life.

I placed signs or plaques with the word *love* in every room in my home. I continued my TV appearances for a local network in the Tampa area speaking about topics such as solar and lunar eclipses, current events, and sports figures.

I quit smoking and started to feel energized and renewed. I decided to springboard my momentum by including daily mediations. I focused on deep breathing to complement my physical exercise and make my body feel great.

It had been five years since I'd put my manuscript in a box. Getting published was unfinished business, and I'd not been able to let it go completely. I knew I'd try to publish again, but I'd lost the motivation and hoped it would come back. I still didn't know if it was the right (divine) time or if the universe was waiting for me to try again. I didn't know if I was to learn patience or perseverance. I wanted to remove myself from a victim mentality, so I said a heartfelt prayer to the universe to help restart my new career again. I took the manuscript out and updated it with recent events.

While cleaning out my inbox, I came across an e-mail promoting a writing contest. The publisher, Balboa Press, was looking for nonfiction work. I registered to join and became instantly motivated to tweak my manuscript. Two weeks after my submission, I had an uncomfortable feeling about it. I felt that it wasn't the correct manifestation, and I hoped that I wouldn't win. And sure enough, when the deadline passed and the winners were announced, I was not one of them.

Since the holidays were fast approaching and I was busy with my job and social life, I temporarily detached from the book. I didn't want too much time to pass and didn't want to lose momentum, so I was happy when the holidays were over.

When 2013 arrived, I rewrote the manuscript one more time. I removed stories that didn't educate or inspire others and eliminated almost one hundred thousand words. I felt inspired to rewrite the book as an educational memoir detailing the events that taught me many lessons and led to my spiritual awakening.

In early March, I revisited Balboa Press's website and saw that they were sponsoring another nonfiction contest. The deadline was two months away, so I registered again and restructured the book. I contacted my friend Judy, an exceptionally talented writer, to review a few chapters and suggest last-minute adjustments. Once completed, I promised myself that I would detach from the outcome. I submitted the manuscript and focused on other aspects in my life.

When the contest was over, I was one of the thirty finalists, but I didn't win any of the top three prizes. I felt a bit of gratification from being a finalist; it meant that my book had been read and garnered interest. I hadn't wanted to self-publish because of time, desire, and money but decided that's exactly what I needed to do—once and for all—so I could get this book out of my system, but first I had to deal with a family issue.

My mother, who had relocated to Puerto Rico, had been recently depressed over the loss of her dogs and had suffered from a major hernia. She felt isolated and expressed her desire to move back to Florida.

Alexis and I agreed to assist her. I flew down to help Mother pack and brought her cats back with me. They lived with me until we found an apartment for Mother and them the following month.

Mother scheduled her hernia surgery for March. I advised her to reschedule it since March was not favorable for surgery except in life-or-death situations, because Mars was retrograde, which could cause complications, as Mars influences our energy levels and affects the body as a whole. She said she couldn't wait any longer and would take her chances.

My anxiety grew each day. I picked her up the morning of her surgery and took a selfie of her and me just in case the worst-case scenario happened. Although Mother and Aunt Nancy had reunited years before, they had typical sibling rivalry and were not close during this period. Mother asked me not to disclose her planned surgery to Aunt Nancy, but I knew better. With my astrology knowledge and the family estrangement behind me, I needed to do the right thing, so I advised Aunt Nancy just in case anything happened. I had little tolerance for family drama and definitely did not want to partake in my family's destructive behavior.

Aunt Nancy lived fifteen minutes from the hospital, so I secretly told her to meet us there so she could see her sister before the operation. Aunt Nancy was waiting in the pre-op area when we arrived. Mother looked surprised but happy to see her sister. I was glad I hadn't listened to her ego and had done the right thing.

The surgeon advised us that the procedure was complicated and could take up to three hours. I gave the doctor and the nurse my contact information and asked that they contact me when Mother was in recovery. I took some last minute photos of Mother and hugged and kissed her. I went back to Aunt Nancy's house during the operation so we could take our minds off the worrying.

Hours passed and we heard nothing. We lit a candle and kept a silent prayer vigil going. Once we ate dinner and six hours had passed, I could no longer wait. I didn't want to call the hospital for fear of bad news, so we drove there to inquire in person. On the ride, I finally received a call from the nurse telling me that Mother was still in recovery. I asked to speak with the doctor but was told that he'd already left. I was upset with the lack of communication and conveyed that to the nurse.

After visiting Mother I felt relieved to see that she had survived. I stayed until almost midnight and then headed home. Unfortunately Mother had complications with her blood pressure and breathing the next day, so she was admitted to the ICU.

During the next two weeks, Mother struggled with the breathing treatments and was very slow to improve. She seemed anxious, sometimes detached, and upset to be alive. I was frustrated at her attitude, and so were the ICU nurses.

Unfortunately Mother had a major setback from a ruptured intestine and was rushed for emergency surgery. The doctor said the surgery would be a minor fix and would last only twenty minutes, but I had an uneasy feeling in my gut. It was another unfavorable day for surgery, but I had to surrender to whatever was her fate. This time, Aunt Nancy and I waited in the hospital lobby and looked at the patient monitor to see when Mother's surgery was over.

We waited and waited, and after another six anxiety-filled hours, her status changed to recovery. The doctor appeared and advised us that her rupture was more complicated than it had appeared and that he'd had to redo the hernia repair as well. He warned that her recovery would be lengthy because of her emphysema.

Aunt Nancy and I finally stepped away to eat dinner. Again, I had an uneasy feeling about Mother's long recuperation and expressed this to Aunt Nancy. I knew Mother's personality well and didn't feel she had the desire to recover. This was serious, so I contacted Alexis, who flew down the next day.

The following week was rough, especially seeing Mother on a ventilator. Alexis stayed the whole week in ICU while I worked during the day and visited most nights. When mother was put on oxygen, she seemed to be speaking to spirits. I didn't know if she was hallucinating from the medication or connecting with the other side until she started to mention names of people who had departed.

Mother's condition declined the following week. Her vitals were erratic, and she voiced her desire to die. She had no more will to live. Within twenty-four hours, Mother was discharged from the hospital and admitted to hospice.

The next day, Mother sat up in bed looking peaceful and seeming lucid. She said, "God removed my burden. All that really matters is love and peace."

Alexis and I stayed at the hospice the last days of her life. The night before Mother passed away, I had the following dream:

I was standing by Mother's bedside, and she leaned over and hugged my waist with both arms to say good-bye. When I looked at her, I was surprised to see that she had no hair and no eyebrows. She looked like an alien.

I woke up and stared at the ceiling. I stood up from the couch and walked over to Mother. She was asleep and still breathing. Her hair and eyebrows were intact. I looked at Alexis, who was also sound asleep on the recliner. I thought it was a strange dream and chalked it up to anxiety, shrugging it off. Mother passed away the following evening.

The week after her death was emotional. I visited many friends and felt amazing support. Music had always healed me, and it was definitely my salvation during this time. Songs speak for feelings. This is why hearing a specific song will trigger a memory. It doesn't matter if a song makes you feel sad or happy—it makes you feel! And expressing feelings, not repressing them, is what matters.

The day of Mother's memorial, I woke up from another strange dream:

Mother was naked and very pregnant. She went into labor and decided to lay on her side, and she delivered a son in front of me. I yelled, "Don't forget to pull the cord out of you!" She said, "Don't worry; everything is fine." She gently pulled the cord from her, and instead of being connected to a placenta, it had two prongs at the end. I was very surprised and woke up.

The dream left me with no emotions. I didn't understand it, so I chalked it up to anxiety again. I got through the memorial and then took Alexis to the airport. She had been away from her husband and pets and looked forward to healing and reconnecting with her family up north.

Although the next month was physically and emotionally draining, I managed to rest and exercise often, and I gained more energy. The next month, I resumed astrology consultations.

In subsequent months, I reminisced about all the ups and downs I had experienced with Mother. I recalled that ten years earlier, I had confronted her about the childhood issues that had bothered me and had learned to forgive her by understanding her childhood and challenges. I also had immense compassion for her. A breast cancer survivor, she had lived through a double radical mastectomy many years before.

I'd worried about her welfare most of my life. I felt that I was the parent and she the child many times. Now I no longer had to worry. I felt a sense of completion instead of devastation.

I took the next few months to repaint and restructure my condo in the evenings. I needed a creative project to channel my grief. In honor of Mother, I'd play the oldies music station, listening to her favorite songs from the fifties and sixties. I often felt her presence while I was doing my home improvements since she had loved building things, a trait she most likely inherited from her father, a carpenter.

One weekend after a long bike ride, I placed my empty water bottle on the kitchen counter. Later that afternoon, I saw the bottle fly off the counter and fall to the floor. I smiled from ear to ear and acknowledged her presence.

The very next weekend, Mother came to me in another dream:

I was standing still and speaking with Mother, amazed to be in her presence. She said, "I'm in Mars or Uranus right now." I said, "But where are you living now?" I waited and waited to hear an address, but she never replied. I woke up with my heart pounding.

This dream finally awakened me to all the traits my dreams about her shared. *Could mother be an alien?*

Was it a coincidence that I'd just started reading Shirley MacLaine's memoir *Out on a Limb* and come across the section that revealed the existence of other entities, or aliens, when I had my third strange dream about Mother?

I hadn't shared any of these dreams with anyone until one evening when I had a video chat with Alexis. I panned the camera around my place to show her my newly painted walls and other home improvements. After we chatted about our pets and jobs, I shared all three dreams with her. I then shared the alien segment of *Out on a Limb* and said, "Alexis, I think our mother is an alien."

Like a scene out of a horror movie, the second after I disclosed my revelation, something crashed behind me. Startled, I stared at Alexis and started to cry. Everything hit me at once. Tears dripped off my chin as I stood there, frozen. Alexis's mouth remained opened in shock.

After I composed myself, Alexis said, "Oh my God, what was that?" She hadn't moved or blinked an eye. I had no idea what had happened, so I decided to investigate. The noise had come from the kitchen, so I opened the pantry and saw that my huge plastic container of pretzels had been knocked off the top shelf and had crashed into the aluminum pantry doors.

I showed Alexis what I'd found. We agreed that Mother had visited and had testified that she was an alien. I believed that, and ever acknowledging it, I haven't had an alien or *strange* dream about her since. That was one heck of a visit.

But Mother's physical death wasn't the only loss I experienced at this time. My employer was selling off part of its retail business, so I was notified that my job was being eliminated in months. I was also notified by the CBS-TV affiliate that after seven years of my astrology appearances, they no longer needed my services.

As all these endings came about, I had quiet, peaceful knowing that everything would be okay. In the past, when I sensed a chapter was about to end, it would bring about anxiety. But life's experiences had taught me not to react with ego. It seemed that I couldn't control these events, but I could control my *reaction* to them, and because of my spiritual awareness and divine connection, I kept the emotions in check and gracefully accepted the endings—*knowing* that a birth, a new beginning, would surface.

CHAPTER FIFTEEN

SURRENDER

I wanted to cocoon for a small period of time, so I stepped away from a few social events and yearly gatherings, including some charity events. I turned to my books for comfort and as a source of knowledge and growth.

A bookmark and highlighter accompanied every book I read, and occasionally I reread highlighted passages and sentences to cement a lesson in my mind. At this time, I made sure to clear my mind of worry and anger and create a space for peace and creativity. Slowing down made me more aware of releasing my ego and any fear and to reclaim joy and excitement. I needed to fully trust in the universe again. I needed to *surrender*—the ultimate spiritual test. Without surrendering, I was silently suffering. I needed to break through the self-limitations that were my undoing. I reread passages from *A Course in Miracles* and *The Law of Attraction* to refocus my mind and allow miracles to unfold. I felt more ready than ever to finally be free—the see true light. Now I know what it feels like to be born again.

Trevor and I went to the beach during a warm fall day. He and I were speaking about our abandonment by our now deceased fathers and how their absences had influenced our lives. We stayed until sunset and then watched the moon shine on the ocean. The sky was clear, and we sat under a bed of stars. It was magical! My consciousness elevated, I felt transposed into another dimension. I felt safe and in peace during my meaningful discussion with Trevor. I could feel the energy of the stars beam down to me and really felt that I was one with them. Since the stars are made of the same energy as us, we are all connected. Our forms may be different, but our essence is the same. I felt the most connected to the universe that beautiful evening. I'd never sat on the beach after nightfall and was captivated by the experience. I now seek solace at the beach on a clear night to remember my connection to this endless source of love.

I'd been drawn to the vibration of numbers since I was a kid. I was especially fascinated with odd numbers, and for no reason I could understand, I'd add up phone numbers, addresses, and birthdays to see if the sum was odd. As my consciousness evolved and I became spiritually awakened, I'd learned that numerology was just one of many tools for understanding our spiritual purposes on earth.

I'd learned that repetition was always a message from the universe. One number pattern that appeared and reappeared almost daily was 555:

I serviced a client at work and noticed the client's address started with 555.

Driving home from the gym one evening, I glanced at the odometer and saw that it read 10,555.

While watching a basketball game one evening, the referee called a TV time-out, and I heard the analyst say that the time remaining in the game was 5:55.

While responding to some e-mails one Saturday, I glanced at the time on the computer and found it was 5:55 in the evening.

I found myself behind a police officer's vehicle driving home from food shopping one evening. When I stopped at a red light, I happened to glance at the police car's license plate and, you guessed it, it included 555.

I continued to see this number pattern in many other places. I texted Trevor one day to asked him his thoughts on this. He said, "The universe is confirming that you're in alignment with your life."

According to *Angel Numbers* by Doreen Virtue and Lynnette Brown, 555 means "major changes and significant transformation are here for you. You have an opportunity to break out of the chrysalis and uncover the amazing life you truly deserve."

I was so glad that both answers were positive and affirming. The universe was speaking to me, and I was paying attention, which is not always easy in our overstimulated state. I was amazed that the universe captured my attention at a precise moment in time to allow me to see numbers to communicate a massage. I felt excited; maybe it was the right time for everything to flow.

I completed my home improvements and celebrated the holidays. I felt more mentally grounded and decided to resume work on my manuscript. I had been away from my dream for too long, but it had never left me! I updated it with recent events and reinstated many stories that I had omitted to conform to the guidelines of the last writer's contest.

I now believe the other manuscripts weren't the correct incarnation and that those hadn't been the right times to publish, but now I had a different outlook. I felt that I had the correct manifestation at the divine time. I burned the midnight oil every night pushing through the tiredness from work to re-edit and tweak the manuscript.

I purchased a self-publishing package from Balboa Press and submitted the manuscript. This time I didn't stress and feel doubt. I knew I'd succeed and looked forward to the wonderful opportunities the universe would bring me. I *surrendered* the outcome to the universe and lived in the present moment of love and peace.

I included a small inspirational section to share further spiritual secrets and more amazing stories.

I close this section with an inspiring story that touched me deeply. My friend Becky treated me to an awesome Fleetwood Mac concert recently. At the end of the show, legendary vocalist Stevie Nicks addressed the audience by expressing her gratitude for the years of support. She shared a passionate story of her dream of becoming a musician one day. She was immensely grateful that after sixteen years away, Christine McVie had rejoined the band to reunite everyone. She ended her speech by urging the audience, "Never ever give up on your dreams!"

THE DIVINE GIFTS

CHAPTER SIXTEEN

DREAMS

Dreams are collections of images and symbols that flood the mind when we are asleep. They reveal our inner worlds and archive our emotional experiences. They are also a channel through which the universe and energy forms communicate with us.

Emotions fuel dreams. When dreams invoke strong emotions, they do so to balance the mind and the heart. They clean out the daily emotional inbox and filter junk from fact. They also express unresolved issues buried in the subconscious.

I started to record myself speaking about my dreams after finding journaling too cumbersome and inconsistent. The purchase of a voice-activated recorder improved my connection to the other side. I began a daily ritual of recording my dreams the moment I woke up. Recording what I call the "afterthought" is important as well. This is documenting your first conscious awareness of what you believe the dream meant the moment you wake. So after you write down or record your dream, document your afterthought as well. This bit of information is unclouded by deep examination and helps you decipher the dream's message.

Some dream messages are clear, vivid, and active, while others leave us feeling confused. Don't despair if you can't clearly understand the message. Relax and ask for another dream. Trust that if the universe has a message, it will come again in another dream or another vehicle.

Repetitive dreams send you a strong message. In one such dream, I was watching reports of a sex scandal on television. It repeated three times within two weeks. Then I had a hunch that my partner at the time was being unfaithful. These messages provided the proof I needed to end a deceptive, unhealthy relationship. I later discovered my hunch was correct, and I'm grateful to the universe for looking out for me.

"Release," or fear-based, dreams can be terrifying and paralyzing, but they bear a lot of fruit. They work overtime to balance our emotions, and they assist us in our healing. Think of the word *fear* as an acronym for *f*rozen *e*motion *a*nd *r*esponse. These dreams can clear out illusions or release fear from our consciousness.

Some dreams are filled with drama and suspense. These devices communicate a strong message and indicate that strong bottled-up emotions are seeking a constructive outlet. If you're warding off an attacker, running from an animal, or swatting away an insect, your unconscious mind is symbolically conquering hidden fears.

Know this: if your dream is negative or frightening, your consciousness is being healed. If you feel discomfort from these dreams, then physical exercise, meditation, prayer, and affirmations can help you release subconscious residue of negativity or fear and bring you relief.

Symbolic dreams are the most common. I've noticed there are personal symbols and universal symbols. Symbols are descriptive tools from the universe's spiritual handbook.

Personal symbols are from your frame of reference—they're specific to you. They vary widely and may include your favorite singer, number, or color. Many personal symbolic dreams involve people from your conscious life: parents, siblings, friends, coworkers. They often represent general concepts that lead to specific personal messages. For example, if your mother appears in a dream, she may represent nurturing, intuition, or emotion. For a basic interpretation, focus on the symbols to extract the main meaning. Then zero in on what the details communicate about your present life.

Universal symbols are archetypal—they are universally shared. Dreaming of your teeth falling out is an example. Generally, this dream represents a fear of change and not a need to visit the dentist. Researching dream symbols in a book or on the Internet can provide you with additional knowledge.

Healing dreams are the ones that make you feel better. They can involve incredible contact with deceased loved ones, including pets, or falling in love or being in a happy relationship. These dreams provide emotional warmth that can linger for hours and leave us in a state of bliss.

Spirit dreams are compelling, vivid, and real. They provide strong healing. These dreams are a common vehicle for spirit communication. Dreams of deceased loved ones have a profound impact on our conscious lives. They teach us one of life's greatest lessons: to let go and live in love.

Spirits with whom you've had strained relationships during their time on earth often use dreams to send messages of love and forgiveness. Use these communications as opportunities to forgive and let go. Healing takes place on earth and in the spirit world. Love is infinite.

Most spirit dreams occur in the middle of your sleep cycle or right before your normal waking time. Utilize these insightful messages on your earthly journey. Share the knowledge with others, especially if the message is universal.

It is a privilege to have spirit dreams. Each one mitigates our fear of the illusion of death and provides us with a powerful message.

If you doubt that your departed loved ones are watching and protecting you, the following dream might offer reassurance. A former coworker named Rita related it to me. This is one of my favorite dreams.

Rita told me that one night, she'd had an argument with her husband. She was so upset at him that after he went to bed, she spitefully hid his eyeglasses in the most obscure place she could find: behind a can of food on the top shelf of the kitchen pantry.

The following morning after she'd gone to work, Rita's husband called and told her that he knew she had secretly hidden his eyeglasses and that he'd already found them in the pantry. Surprised, she wondered, *How did he know I hid his eyeglasses? I thought he would assume he had misplaced them*, and she asked him these questions. He replied, "My deceased twin brother came to me in a dream right before I woke up and revealed that you'd hidden my glasses in the pantry." Rita was stunned. She apologized to her husband and now thinks twice about seeking revenge.

Precognitive dreams, also called "clairvoyant" or "premonition" dreams, provide insight into and preparation for future events. They strongly confirm that there is a divine script.

Once the portal for such dreams is opened, premonitions of many events—both good and not so good—enter your dreams. The good premonition dreams give us insight to aid others or ourselves in the progression of life. They can generate hope and anticipation for an impending positive event. I have had many dreams predicting pregnancies for friends and colleagues, sometimes even with the baby's gender. Another colleague, Julia, was a common subject of my premonition dreams. I dreamt about all three of her pregnancies, including one that ended in miscarriage.

This brings me to the flip side of precognitive dreams: if your premonitions are difficult, they can create worry and anxiety. Only you can decide if you want to handle the responsibility of knowing what will happen. You also have the power to specifically state what you can and cannot handle. The universe hears your thoughts, requests, and prayers. Be specific, and your wishes will be honored.

Once I became conscious of this spiritual entryway, I experienced the good and the not so good. Tragic premonitions were a challenge. The following are two disturbing dreams that led me to take charge and determine my boundaries:

- Police officers were chasing two men driving a stolen vehicle. The high-speed chase ended when the two men lost control and crashed into a wooden fence. They were instantly decapitated.
- A man was standing on the top rung of a ladder doing some repairs on the outside of his home. I then witnessed him fall to the ground and heard his hip shatter in my head.

These dreams were disturbing, but then the validations came: I heard on the evening news that two men had died tragically in a car crash during a police chase. Soon after, while walking through a hallway at work, I overheard a conversation between two men discussing another coworker's recent accident. While doing outside home repairs, he had fallen from a ladder and broken his hip.

But I'd already decided I couldn't handle any more traumatizing premonitions. After waking from the shattered-hip dream, I immediately demanded to the universe, "Please stop these dreams! Only give me premonitions for those I know and those I can help!" This request was immediately answered. I learned that I could set boundaries with the other side. I no longer dream about strangers dying tragically, although I still occasionally get messages of possible illness and miscarriages happening to those I know. I have honored my responsibility to deliver these messages to their recipients, and I've done so with grace.

Taking time to build a relationship with your inner world is both rewarding and exciting. You will discover a whole other realm of knowledge. Remember to get enough rest, and I wish you many sweet dreams.

Suggestions

- Purchase a dream journal or a small audio recorder to record your dreams. Keep it in your bedroom.
- Before you fall asleep, pray to the universe to help you remember your dreams upon waking.
- Record your dreams and the immediate afterthoughts first thing in the morning.
- Treat yourself to an occasional nap. Your dreams are more lucid in the afternoon, as you can remember dreams more vividly because you're unconscious for less time. Record these dreams as well.
- Listen to or read your dream recordings periodically, on a schedule that works for you—every few days, weeks, or even months. Eventually, you will notice some patterns and similarities. This exercise will also help you to differentiate universal symbols from your personal symbols. Be aware of the signs and answers to your questions and prayers.
- Act upon repetitive dreams that provide a clear directive for your life.

CHAPTER SEVENTEEN

HEALING

Psychologists have identified three main stages of healing from any loss: First is shock and denial, second is anger and depression, and third is understanding and acceptance. Ultimately, loss is temporary since nothing is ever lost in the end. We return home (to spirit form) once we graduate from earth school (from physical form).

Learning to heal is an important process for living a healthy and joyful life on earth. When you choose to heal from any loss, you gain confidence, strength, and freedom from mental turmoil and emotional pain. When you experience multiple losses or a traumatic experience, it is normal to feel overloaded, depressed, and fragile.

It is important to take the time to heal and love ourselves so emotions don't become amplified in the future from repressed grief. Identify the source of emotional pain, and acknowledge that you are in touch with your feelings. Devote a little time each day to your pain. This conscious devotion lets you know that you're not in denial but in touch with the reality of your loss. Ask the universe to assist you with your lessons, and more importantly, ask it to remove the pain.

The mind is moldable, and focusing on acknowledgement of your experience will benefit you tremendously by allowing you to live your daily routine.

The moment you choose to heal, your energy focuses on the healing process, which is exactly that—a process—and not something that will happen overnight. However, your awareness of spiritual truth and of your thoughts helps you get through the loss sooner.

You may experience setbacks and slip into victim mode and anger while you're healing. Don't despair; this is normal but not *real*. The mind wanders when it's not focused, and the ego loves to play the victim, allowing negative and painful scenarios to surface. Loss can also trigger fears, insecurities, and unresolved issues. Don't buy into this mental drama. It will pass. Know too that it's impossible to be completely focused all the time. But I've gone from one extreme emotion to another by virtue of awareness, or changing my thoughts. I've gone from negative to positive and despair to peace in seconds—it really works!

When you feel pain, you may find it helpful channel that energy to do something constructive or creative. Forgive another, write a book, talk a friend's ear off, or do whatever you feel compelled to do as long as it's constructive and creative.

For example, musicians often express their pain through music. This outlet is one of the best expressions of feelings ever created, and others reap the benefits of their emotional journeys. Songs can describe pain, joy, or and the rapture of love and salvation. You may not be a recording artist, but we are all musicians in our hearts, so sing whatever song that makes you feel better.

Rewriting this book over and over again was extremely cathartic for me. Although some memories were painful to write about, doing so often helped me cope with residual resentment and negative feelings.

Make sure you do communicate your feelings in whatever creative expression you choose. To have a healthy mind and heart, we must get out painful thoughts and feelings. Do not fear your pain. Use it as a learning opportunity to expand your awareness of love, life, and liberation. Face it, and feel it the best way possible. There is no race and no finish line for getting through a loss. It's good to be in touch with your feelings. Heal at your own speed, love yourself, and you will recover!

Guilt is an emotion that can surface from a loss. It is an aspect of the ego as it tries to make you stay in victim mode. If you feel sad or regretful about a statement or deed toward a deceased loved one, you can move through this feeling and not lament over it. We are on earth to learn, and sometimes the lessons are tough.

If you acknowledge a sad or painful memory of an unsavory statement or deed, this is the opportunity to tell yourself that you did the best you could at the time. Remember, if we misbehave, we do so because we allow our egos to rule. You can only act or react from your current feelings, so let guilt pass and feel compassion for your actions instead. Every soul knows that all of us on earth are learning and growing, and the awareness of your past painful experiences is the key to healing them now, to living more peacefully in the present.

Grief is different for everyone. It can take on many faces: endless tears, physical exhaustion, psychological turmoil, depression. These feelings are natural and normal, and best of all, temporary.

After an astrology session one evening, I asked my sixty-three-year old client, "What words of wisdom can you share with me?" She smiled and said, "It doesn't matter how bad your day's been, find something to laugh at, and enjoy every day."

You can feel joy and optimism within sadness and despair. Keeping your life simple and laughing when you can keeps you connected to your true self.

Laughing provides one of the greatest energy boosts we can give ourselves. I often advise my clients that, crying opens the heart, but laughing heals it. Have you ever noticed how intense and heartfelt laughter is when you're hurting and healing? The late author Norman Cousins attributed daily doses of belly laughter to part of his recovery from life-threatening collagen disease early in his life. Enjoy great laughs every chance you get.

My Story

I allowed myself to go through the stages of healing after the death of my mother. I was out of my body the first month, but I felt more myself in subsequent months, and I tried to get enough sleep to heal my emotions. I reached out to friends who had lost parents, and their stories comforted me. Many told me that they never got *over* the loss of a parent completely, but they did get *through* the loss.

Meditation, physical exercise, counseling, and constructive projects helped my energy level increase. Although some days, such as birthdays, anniversaries, and holidays, triggered tears, the sadness came less frequently, and her visits also comforted me.

Compassion

Compassion is born when two or more souls are united in emotional support. Whenever you are healing from any loss, take time to listen to others, as listening is an form of compassion. We are all the same when we feel pain or are healing from losses. A rich man who breaks his leg will feel the same physical pain as the poor man who breaks his. The same goes for a rich woman and a poor woman going through natural childbirth. Your social status, material wealth, and physical appearance will not mitigate pain. Compassion is a high vibration of love—it illuminates loving energy and reconnects us with the spirit of humanity, since we are all one.

Emotional Pain

Emotional pain is energy that we can harness to transform our lives. It wakes us up and trains us to be more alert at all times. To feel is part of the earthly experience, and feelings exist so that we may experience sensations that in turn expand our awareness.

Emotional pain is temporary, and aren't we grateful for that! When you feel pain, use it to better your life and to serve others, because the quicker you can use pain for constructive ends, the sooner it fades and leads to greater clarity. Some losses are more difficult to get through, so you may feel emotional pain for longer than you'd like. These deep emotional experiences are usually life transforming. Acknowledge your feelings, and understand that the pain will pass.

In my eyes, emotional pain is the worst feeling and the driving force for so much more despair. Emotional pain can drive someone to snap or overreact. Haven't we all said something in haste when we were hurting emotionally, only to apologize for having created more hurt?

Expressing emotions constructively is important! Shedding tears does help to relieve the pain and balance the mind. Suppressing feelings can leave you numb, distant, angry, depressed, and lost. Repressed emotions can turn into physical ailments. Repression is just not worth it. The ego loves to play the victim and loves to dwell in drama. Living in that state is exhausting and a waste of time. I'd rather go dancing or out to dinner with friends. Laughter and tears are polar expressions, but they both constructively *express* feelings.

I was having a deep discussion with a close friend about a heavy-hearted relationship I was experiencing. I was trying to let go of my emotional attachment and subsequent pain. My friend gracefully reminded me, "I know earth is a schoolroom and you're trying to learn a lesson, but you're taking this too seriously. Remember that schools have playgrounds and time for recess. Don't be so hard on yourself." I immediately laughed and felt relieved. I needed to follow my own advice.

Living in any kind of emotional pain for extended periods of time is not noble. There is no award for the person who has the highest pain tolerance. Although we have all suffered for fear of letting something or someone go, doing so eventually wears us down until the ego has no more energy. Short-term suffering is common, but long-term suffering is unnecessary. Spiritual growth is the only purpose for emotional pain. Healing emotional pain gives you a great appreciation for life, joy, and love.

Forgiveness

Forgiveness is empowering! Forgiveness is another divine gift of healing. It is emancipation from anything that caused you pain. It is not condoning the conscious or unconscious behavior that caused pain but detaching your energy from it and rising above it. It is easier to forgive when we understand *why* a situation happened than when we don't understand. If someone did something to hurt you, he or she must be in pain. If you have issues with people in or out of your life, try to forgive them.

Start with family, and then move on to friends, ex-lovers, bosses, and coworkers. If you don't have any trouble forgiving, then you're lucky—or visiting from another planet. (And if you are visiting from another planet, please drop this book and get back on your spaceship.)

Anger is a strong response to pain, and it requires a lot of energy. It is fueled by will and determination, so choose to express it constructively. At times when I'm angry, I'd turn up the volume in my car radio and sing along at the top of my lungs. Finding a safe place to yell and scream can help release anger. Forgiveness will get you through your anger. This is not the easiest lesson to learn but one of the most valuable. Give it a try and see how you feel. If you don't succeed at first, try and forgive again, later. Your energy is precious, so use it lovingly.

Lack of forgiveness creates resentment, a trap that subconsciously leads us to disappointment, detrimental actions, and sustained emotional pain. Resentment can be cured by forgiveness, therefore clearing precious mental space for love, peace, and harmony.

There are many ways to forgive, including through time, understanding, and present awareness.

Forgiveness through time is the most common, especially if you've gone through a breakup or divorce. During the healing period, find creative outlets, and stay focused on your personal interests. Remember to have fun and laugh often. With time, emotional pain subsides until we are no longer obsessed with the wrongdoing or separation. When we have created a new routine and feel more at peace with ourselves, we tend to let go of the negative viewpoint of another.

Forgiveness from understanding is probably the most gratifying of all. When we can see negative patterns or behaviors in ourselves, we tend to more easily recognize these in others. Since we want to be forgiven and loved when we've messed up, we have to do the same for others. When I understood the patterns my parents had passed on to me, I forgave my parents for all the unsavory choices that impacted me and released the expectations or illusions I held them to. I became mindful of changing the pattern.

Forgiveness given from present awareness is the quickest way to peace. A few years back, I was in the early stages of dating a very attractive guy when he suddenly cancelled our plans for the night after confirming them only thirty minutes earlier. I was deeply upset, and I stewed for a couple of weeks before I cooled off. Then one afternoon, as fate would have it, I was writing a segment on forgiveness.

I felt uneasy and couldn't continue to write, because I still harbored anger toward him. I hadn't forgiven him yet. So I decided to meditate and relax to refocus. During my mediation, I heard my inner voice say, "Martin, do you want to be right, or do you want peace?" I immediately got it! I became giddy and light-hearted. That the ego wanted to be right but the soul needed to do the right thing was the *true* battle. It wasn't the action that really mattered; it was my reaction that would settle the whole matter. I danced out of my meditation room feeling renewed and happy. It didn't matter what he did; I had chosen to have peace from it, and I regained my authentic self. I thanked the universe for the awesome revelation.

Harboring resentment is like having our mental roots clogged by the water made murky by accumulated anger and pain. Let go of these rotted roots and give yourself a break. You deserve to be happy and in peace, and you attain this state by letting go of resentment. Just the awareness that you're angry at someone can help you change your energy to a more positive emotion. You may not *feel* like forgiving, but if you think about it, you'll start the process.

Another magical by-product of forgiveness is the blessings it provides to you and to others without your conscious awareness. Whenever you choose to forgive another, you will feel healed. The energy will cosmically boomerang back to you because we all share one consciousness. You honor yourself by releasing this toxic energy and helping others grow. You possess the power to heal.

My astrological research shows that many healers and spiritual teachers have forgiveness as a major theme in their spiritual blueprints. They have had to go through many painful times, including challenging childhoods. Releasing these painful experiences helped them to shed layers of doubt and fear from their lives. Forgiveness emancipated them from their internal barriers.

Self-forgiveness is equally important for healing whenever you've overreacted or said something to cause another pain. Self-honesty is a doorway to personal growth and great rewards. It is okay to feel bad about an unsavory choice, but don't dwell or lament on it. Correct it as soon as possible. When you view your mistakes as learning experiences, you can lovingly correct them and not punish yourself or allow the experiences to defeat you. Acts of self-forgiveness build your self-esteem while keeping you humble.

Practicing forgiveness opens your heart to reveal the endless mass of your soul. Your capacity to forgive is enormous—endless—because your soul is part of the essence of unconditional love.

Forgiveness is fabulous, fantastic, faith-filled, fashionable, favorable, fearless, feasible, fervent, festive, finalizing, fine, firm, and foolproof. It is also forceful, forever, frank, freeing, fruitful, fueling, and *soul*-fulfilling.

Growth

Growing pains lead to real growth. We all had to experience physical growing pains when we were children, especially during adolescence. In order to spur new growth in our plants, we often have to trim them back.

Growth always triggers change, and it can bring in new friends, careers, even a new physical appearance. You can't but change from a loss, especially psychologically. When we view losses as having purpose, we no longer see them in vain. It doesn't matter how unsettling the change, please know that you are much wiser for the experience.

The spiritual growth that comes from healing is another great cosmic gift. Spiritual growth comes when you allow your consciousness to shift to a higher vibration—to a spiritual outlook on life, where you see yourself as a student. When you feel healed and have made the psychological change to view loss spiritually, you gain mental freedom, which is empowering. The great gift of loss is the impetus to live!

Physical Death

Healing from the physical death of a loved one is a process we all experience. It is part of our spiritual growth. Though we miss the physical presence, touch, and voice of a loved one, losing them births or rebirths our spiritual beliefs. Death is a transition from one dimension to another. Both the newly departed and the physical survivors learn from the transition. One of the lessons is that love is an energy that transforms but never dies.

Those in spirit learns to communicate to the physical survivors through energy by manipulating light fixtures, appliances, and other electrical devices. Spirits also communicate through dreams, songs, and many other creative resources, including butterflies and birds.

The physical survivor learns to be receptive to such occurrences and to understand that energy lives on in a new form. This lesson confirms that bonds of love never end and that we can live without fear of death. Also, we no longer have to worry or feel responsible for the physically deceased; they are now in a safer dimension.

Some physical losses are tougher and more painful than others. Such losses can leave a profound impact on your life, and the experience can help you grow the most. When significant losses grip your existence, you may have to experience multiple healing methods to recover. You may want to journal or speak to many people who will lend an ear. Meditate, exercise, or treat yourself to a full body massage. Whatever you do, trust that you will recover.

Although the physical body is temporary, the spirit that resides there is eternal. To heal from physical death, we must perceive the transition as a spiritual truth. Physical death is a graduation from the spirit body in *physical* form to the spirit body in *spirit* form. As we surrender our attachment to our loved ones in their physical form, let us smile through the tears, for they are reunited with family members—including pets—who transcended before them.

Broken Relationships

Healing from broken relationships is similar to healing from a physical death. In some cases, the emotional pain is even more acute, since the grief is for the living and not the deceased. Sometimes it hurts just to breathe deeply. It can seem unfair that we feel so much pain, yet the other person is still physically alive. Sometimes closure seems more elusive after the demise of a relationship.

However, an emotional loss carries the same weight whether it involves a person's death or a relationship's death. Emotions are a part of our makeup, and our souls grow through our hearts' experiences. Such a loss is an opportunity to acknowledge the hurt, to learn the lessons, and to focus on what you do want in a partner and in life.

Everyone reacts and heals differently. Remember that you will become stronger through this experience. When the time is right, you will be in a healthier relationship with the right person.

Truth

When we tell the truth, our eyes radiate innocence from our souls. At times, telling the truth can make us feel vulnerable, but doing so is necessary for healing. Honesty breeds credibility, makes you a stronger person, and helps you tell the truth more easily next time. Conscious behavior forms habits, so speaking the truth is living in love. Truth is a lesson that truly freed my mind and heart. It is the gateway to the house of redemption and peace. It builds character and trust.

Nontruths are detrimental to your relationships. When I finally met my dad at the age of eight, the damage of not knowing him had already been done, especially subconsciously. When relationships are strained by many years of nontruth, secrets, and doubt, they are further strained by the fear that coming clean might only make things worse. This fearful mind-set keeps many holding on to unhealthy and painful relationships because they believe that a toxic relationship is better than estrangement.

Although the truth may cause estrangement in some cases, it will *always* benefit everyone in the long run because it allows wounds to finally heal cleanly, spurring for new growth and possibilities. When I was aware enough to see my abandonment clearly, I saw the truth that my dad was caught up in a cycle of estrangement.

Court witnesses are sworn in with their right hands held high or with their hands on the Bible as they promise to tell the truth. In modern society, our ability to live in truth is tested daily. We are given a multitude of communication forums—e-mail, phone correspondence, texts, and face-to-face encounters—to speak the truth to our parents, partners, siblings, children, friends, and coworkers.

Truth is our natural state. Truth and peace are *heaven* on earth—lies and guilt are *hell* on earth. The more truth you give out, the more trust you get in return, for giving and receiving are one.

Truth allows your aura to vibrate at a high level and therefore to attract like-minded truthful souls to your magnetic field. Truth mitigates negativity from our choices and experiences. Open the doors of endless possibilities for love by being truthful. Power lies in truth. Honesty does not cost money, so be a cosmic freeloader and tell the truth.

You can heal anything with an open mind and an honest heart. Truth creates a precedence of optimism for future and current relationships. Correcting a nontruth with spiritual truth is rewarding. Having a freed conscious is priceless—it even allows you to sleep better!

A physically intimate relationship may be a particularly evident outlet for the truth. Relationships demand truth if they are to remain happy and healthy. Some of my friends have been in unhappy and unhealthy relationships and have looked for the perfect excuse to end their of entrapment. A few have asked me how I ended my past relationships. I replied, "I told them the truth." They feared that confronting the truth would be too difficult and hurtful. But the truth is, we are part of the same cosmic consciousness. so if we lie to another, we are lying to ourselves. Honesty is liberating, and it doesn't have to be mean or hurtful.

You were created as a unique individual with the energy of love inside you. You don't need anybody's approval to be happy, so live your truth, and watch the universe bless you with miracles.

The truth can sometimes be a message for another to heal a misperception. The universe has a creative way of bringing us to knowledge and truth. Sometimes we are led to listen to or overhear a conversation for this purpose. I've been led to many books that have expanded my awareness, taught me lessons, and revealed universal truths. We are instruments for assisting each other, so the more truthful we are, the more receptive we become, and the more fulfilled we feel.

Live well, be truthful, and enjoy the rewards of honesty. Be in your present state of awareness, and live with your power, your divine center of spiritual joy. To quote the late abolitionist and activist Elizabeth Cady Stanton, "Truth is the only safe ground to stand upon."

The truth is that love doesn't have a gender, religion, or nationality. It is the essence within, and we all possess it. The truth is that life is more bearable, joyful, and empowering, when we function from pure awareness. The truth liberates, educates, and heals.

Suggestions

- Take time to be patient with yourself. Add thyme to your spice cabinet, and include it in your meals. Plant the seeds and grow some thyme.
- Have a candlelight dinner with yourself. Cook or order in— just make sure your meal is delicious and nurturing.
- Reach out for help. Google "counseling support" for individual or group counseling.
- Keep a couple of journals. Place one in your bag or briefcase, and keep another at home. Write whenever you feel like it: during your lunch break, on public transportation, or while during commercial breaks from a TV show. When some time has passed and you feel strong enough, go back and read some of the passages you've written. Use this exercise to gauge your healing and growth. Your current consciousness will surprise you.
- Laugh, laugh, laugh. Go to a comedy club. Buy a joke book, and share the laughter with a friend. Start with this one, which I created about my own life: "I have been through so many growing experiences that I started naming my stretch marks."
- Go to a zoo. Animals give out unconditional love and healing energy. Adopt a pet that fits your lifestyle.
- Visit a botanical garden or nature trail.
- Travel. Go to a resort. Swim in the ocean, and enjoy the beach. You can grieve anywhere. Why not cry in the ocean?
- Head for a higher elevation. If you live near a mountain, climb it. If not, travel to a national or state park or a ski resort. Stand or sit on a rock on top of any mountain. Feel your proximity to the heavens, and ask for healing energies to pour over you. I have done this after many losses. Mountains have wonderful healing abilities.
- Read inspirational books on how others have coped with losses.

- Never ever underestimate the power of prayer, regardless of your theological background. Lean on your spiritual foundation. This is a wonderful time to grow in your faith.
- Clean your entire home. Eliminating clutter clears the mind and heals emotions. Go through your cabinets, pantry, closets, refrigerators, freezers, and garages, and create new space in your life.
- Seek out support from female family members or your friends. The emotional resources women can provide are priceless.
- Listen to your favorite music. Let the words and vibrations speak for your soul. Play a song repeatedly, especially if it heals you. While I was healing, I listened to many songs hundreds of times. It works. Also, sing out loud in front of a mirror. Expressing yourself while looking into your eyes is empowering!
- Make a list of fun things to do, and include others to participate. Creating joy and connecting with others make loss bearable.
- Be a friend, and lend your support to someone else.
- Write your autobiography, especially if you have old scars to heal, even if you choose not to publish it. Writing can bring catharsis.

CHAPTER EIGHTEEN

CHOICE

We are all cut from the same cloth and have the spark of love within, but the way we demonstrate the spark varies. Embracing and expressing our individuality is a choice, and no two people, even identical twins, are the same.

For instance, your voice is a magical instrument that separates you from everyone. It can be the voice of a song, lover, or baby that communicates thoughts and expresses emotions that vibrate with other souls. When you look back at a deceased celebrity, movie star, or musician, isn't it that person's voice that distinguishes him or her? Mimicking that uniqueness is what celebrity impersonators truly strive for. Looking like a celebrity is one thing, but sounding like one is what captivates an audience. You never know what legacy your voice will leave on earth. Do not let your voice be silent—choose to use it with love, passion, and your unique style.

Now in our overstimulated world, more than ever, we need to be conscious in our waking life in order to make sound choices. Living with a clear mind and conscious connection to your center will bring favorable results. If you feel out of balance, try to eliminate static from your life.

Choose to surround yourself with positive people, or what I call SIRE people: those who *support, inspire, respect*, and *energize* you. As everyone does, you possess these attributes, and it's important that you uncover these gifts. By using and living in these qualities, you attract the same vibrations from others because of the universal law of attraction.

Choice gives you the power to accept only love and harmony and to transcend everything else. If you suffer from low self-esteem, you can change it. If you had a rotten childhood, you need not have a rotten adulthood. If you feel that you came into this life with excess baggage, you can unload it. If you want to understand your parents, learn about their parents. Many unconscious patterns are repeated from generation to generation. The cycle is waiting to be broken, so choose to break it. We all possess the power to heal and change, but it takes a conscious *choice* to do so.

Do not buy into the idea that ignorance is bliss. It is not easier to stay stuck in horrible situations. Unconscious behavior leads to painful consequences, such as accidents, hurt feelings, and illness. When you realize the difference between your true self (your spiritual self) and your false self (your ego self), you can choose to make positive change. When you choose to become aware, you experience less pain. Choose to change—it becomes your savior.

Your childhood is your foundation. If that foundation has many cracks, it needs to be patched up. All surfaces have scratches and scars; these are a normal consequence of living in the physical world. Skin wrinkles, car paint fades, and shoes wear out. But it's never too late to choose to heal a wound or patch up a crack in your life.

Obstacles and cycles educate us. When you find yourself in a challenging situation time after time, ask why you're in it. This process can be very frustrating, but there is a reason for it. When you are fully aware of that reason, you will think, feel, and see the situation completely. You can then connect the dots and understand the subconscious attitude or behavior that continues the cycle, and you can make wiser choices. Awareness starts the process of healing. You will no longer be a victim of self-destruction, and that is freedom!

Choice is a gift. It does not force you to do anything—you can choose to do nothing or to do something. You can grow and learn if you choose to stretch, strive, and step through the obstacles, which are the avenues to success. Like all of us, you are both student and teacher. As a student you can choose to receive and learn, and as a teacher you can choose to give and teach others.

Liking and loving yourself is a also choice. You can learn to like and love yourself with self-discipline and self-honesty. Haven't you felt good when you've obeyed your intuition or stood by your values?

Your reaction to anything that happens to you is a choice. If an event has caused you stress, you can choose to do something creative or constructive, or surrender what you can't control to the universe.

Another way to view this is through the eyes of an athlete. The incorrect call of an umpire or referee can sway the outcome of a ballgame. Players have the choice to behave with sportsmanship or to react otherwise. I have witnessed many teams initially react with anger to an incorrect call but quickly regain composure and focus and bring about a favorable outcome.

Positive attitudes and behaviors are choices. Before celebrities flew private jets, they flew in commercial airliners. A couple of my senior-flight-attendant friends have shared many stories about the rude attitudes and behaviors of celebrity passengers. I've silently observed that the attendants never comment on the celebrity's physical appearance, career, or wealth—but they do comment on that person's attitude and behavior.

We have many choices—to be happy or sad, to sing or to sulk, to dress sexy or frumpy. We choose what to eat, what soap to use, and what thread count we want for our bedding. When the traffic light shines red, it's our choice to stop. We make so many choices that it's mind-boggling.

On the morning of my thirty-sixth birthday, I woke up thinking about what would make this day special. I went to the beach when I wanted to, I ate out when I wanted to, and I did what I enjoyed, every day. I couldn't think of anything I wanted to do on that day, because I had already chosen to live every day like it was my birthday. And in truth, every day is the *birth* of a new day. Choose to celebrate life every day.

Temptation is part of the journey—how else can you learn to choose what's right for you? It's all part of building character. Remember: it's only a mistake if you don't learn from it. If you punish yourself, you punish others, but if you love yourself, you love others. As within, so without. Always remember that you always have divine assistance, but the power of choice is yours.

Courage

Courage is a liberating quality to develop. By doing or experiencing, we gain confidence. It's like learning to drive a car. The more you drive, the more experience you gain, and the more confidence you feel. Living on earth takes a lot of courage, because an important lesson we learn in our earthly schoolroom is to feel emotions and not fear them. When you experience the first of anything that's painful, such as a breakup or death, dealing with it is initially challenging because your emotions sense the newness of the experience, we fear the unknown. It takes courage to heal, and even more to know you can survive. The more we experience, the more courage we gain. A woman who wants to conceive a second child already knows she will experience severe pain during birth, but knows she can survive it. If it weren't for the courage of women, many of us wouldn't have siblings.

Many fears are stepping stones for character development, or conscious awareness. They are academic courses in courage. If you fear intimacy, you can channel it toward deep, committed love. Doing so requires a humble and honest self-appraisal to uncover the hidden, or subconscious, attitude or block and then find the courage to conquer it. Love heals everything.

Love is the strongest and most creative force in this world. When we believe we are love, then we have the courage to express love, and that's the greatest gift we can give others. And the universe will return what you give. When you have the courage to feel and express love, you liberate others to do the same. We can change the world for the better simply by having the courage to love.

It also takes courage to accept that life's challenges are teaching you valuable lessons. When you courageously accept the role of student, you empower yourself to view obstacles spiritually, and you create a platform to teach others. What good are your lessons if you don't share them with others? More than likely, challenges, if handled courageously, will lead you to happiness and fulfillment. Divine assistance provides the tools and paves the path. All you need to do is activate your free will and allow the universe to use you as an instrument of light for the world's benefit.

When you walk in spiritual awareness, you walk through imaginary walls created by fear and gain momentum to live a fearless life. Confronting fear allows your confidence to soar. When I gave my first radio appearance, I felt so nervous that I silently called out for Archangel Michael for courage. I forged ahead and didn't allow fear to get the better of me. I was so happy and energized from the successful show that I wanted to do another right after. Courage is like a spiritual drug—when you know that fear doesn't really exist, you want to conquer the world. You can succeed in your spiritual mission on earth because courage is a form of love, and love is everlasting.

It takes courage to surrender anger, pain, guilt, fear, or anything else blocking you from experiencing peace. It takes courage to let go. Your courage allows you to make choices that will change your life for the better.

Change

Change is a natural state of the soul's evolution. It is a tool of liberation. Empowered change is imminent when we are conscious and educated, as awareness plus knowledge equals power. You can change a belief, dream, or thought to ensure a different outcome.

When we were young, we eagerly looked forward to the end of the school day, being promoted to the next grade, and growing old enough to make our own choices. All change is a natural state in the flow of life—the weather changes, flowers change, and our bodies change.

We change clothes (hopefully daily), eat different foods, drive different cars, read different books, and interact with different people. If we're to get the most out of life, we must experience many changes. Although stability allows us to establish roots, to create a foundation to build upon, change keeps our lives from getting stagnant and rusty. Change is necessary when things are no longer functioning, especially if we're suffering by holding on to the old or the past. May you flow with change when it's necessary and embrace the variety that earth offers.

Courage, choice, and change are attributes of free will. Courage is taking action in the face of fear, choice is the conscious awareness that you have the power to use free will constructively, and change is allowing your soul to reach a new state in its evolution.

Suggestions

- Choose to learn something every day.
- Choose love—that's all that matters in the end.
- Choose to smile every day and to believe in miracles.
- Choose to embrace your life and your creative talents.
- Success is a choice, so choose to embrace, relish, and lavish in your light.
- Live in choice, courage, and change.

CHAPTER NINETEEN

SIGNS

Coincidences are divine signs that can guide our lives. *Déjà vu* is French for "already seen" and is a common occurrence. It is the reenactment of the physical experience of a spiritual memory that was scripted before our earthly incarnation. It seems familiar because the spirit is recalling the initial mental imprint unconsciously while it experiences the same circumstances consciously.

Déjà vu affirms that you are on your path, following your map. An extended lack of déjà vu can signal a deeply spiritual period, a time of introspection and reconnection to your true essence.

Most signs are subtle and come about without effort, just like longstanding friendships that just happen to form. Signs also surface without our conscious control—they emerge simply from living consciously.

When I prepared to write this book, I felt guided to place paper and pens in every room to capture spontaneous childhood memories or spiritual wisdom. Once, I even had an inspiration while waiting on line for an available bank teller. I didn't have a pen and paper handy, so I stepped out of line, walked to the other end of the bank, and wrote the message on the back of a blank deposit slip. I received another thought while driving one day, so I turned off the radio and listened to the information in my mind. At a stoplight, I wrote my thoughts on the pad I kept on the passenger seat.

The more conscious I became, the more messages were bestowed upon me. Messages and wisdom flooded my mind throughout my waking hours, especially during meditations and while reading books. Once I cleared the meaningless drama from my mind, I created additional space for inspiration.

I pay attention to dreams, books, and numbers, so these were the vehicles that the universe used to communicate to me.

Ever since I could count, I'd been fascinated by numbers. As I was nearing the end of the first draft of this book, I started seeing 1:11 on digital clocks. It didn't matter what room I was in, I'd be guided to look at the clock at the precise moment when it read 1:11.

I then noticed this number everywhere I went. While dining out in Santa Fe, New Mexico, I noticed the restaurant's address was 111. Driving back to the airport, I saw a huge billboard promoting the mega lottery jackpot valued at 111 million dollars. While running on a treadmill, I randomly glanced down to see how far I had run, and the mileage read 1.11 miles. One afternoon, while watching tennis, I looked up at the scoreboard to see the clocked speed of a player's serve: 111 miles per hour.

My angel numbers book said that 111 is a divine sign to declare what I desired from the universe and to make sure my mind focused on only positive thoughts and manifestations. I was amazed at how the universe was guiding me.

Afterlife

Although your loved ones may have departed physically, they are alive and well in spirit. Their visits and signs help you heal from their physical departures. Almost immediately, when a spirit has crossed over and is adjusted to its new environment, it reaches out to friends and family members to let its loved ones know it has made it and is okay. Very often, it reaches out to receptive family or friends—those sensitive to signs—to relay messages.

Many have confirmed that spirits initially communicate through dreams, but spirits can also communicate through electrical items: blinking lights on equipment or appliances, spontaneous powering off of the TV or radio, or any other signals from electronics that are out of the ordinary. Sometimes these signs occur when you're talking or thinking about the one who has just departed, making the visit more profound.

Please don't *expect* signs every time you say or think a name, especially right after a loved one's physical departure. A lack of communication doesn't mean spirits aren't around you. Keep in mind that it takes *energy* to manipulate electricity. When you experience a close physical death, the person or animal seems to consume your thoughts and life for some time. It would be maddening if they constantly flicked the lights and turned on appliances every time you thought or spoke of them.

In subsequent years, signs may fade or change due to natural evolution and expansion. Physical survivors grieve, heal, and grow, and life continues in a different form for our departed loved ones. In fact, the signs you receive from them may change because they are evolving or ascending. As time goes on, they may impress you in innovative, imaginative, or humorous ways to say hello.

I Feel You

As a strongly clairsentient person, I'm receptive to signs from the other side. I experience many sensations whenever I'm in the presence of a spirit guide, angel, or deceased loved one—including pets. Sometimes, I feel a shift in consciousness, light-headedness, or a pressure change in the air around my head. Other times I get an overwhelming feeling of calm and peace. Sometimes I feel a change in the room temperature. I find the presence of all spirit beings comforting.

On the Mark

While studying for my astrology diploma, I found myself utterly frustrated by the many formulas and scientific diagrams. I nearly quit completely on two separate occasions. Yet, both times, messages from the universe surfaced to remind me that I needed to complete my studies.

First, at a friend's birthday party, a stranger walked up to me and struck up a conversation about astrology. Then while I was dining with a friend and his buddies in Chicago, I "guessed" all of their zodiac signs, even though I hadn't met them. Then I remembered the earlier signs that had led me to enroll in the first place: winning the bid for a free astrology report at a silent auction, a coworker's referral to an astrologer, and Alexis introducing this great science to me as a teen. I decided to stick it out, and when I passed all my courses and received my diploma, I was glad I hadn't given up.

Mental Magic

We all experience signs. Many people have sensed an event before it happened. People often cite ESP, or extrasensory perception, as the means. An example of this is when a person suddenly comes to mind seconds before you receive a phone call or correspondence from them. Since we are all energy forms, telepathic messages are easily transmuted and assimilated. We can't escape it—it's the highest and most natural form of communion.

While meditating early one morning, I received a vision of two old friends from New York that I hadn't heard from in months. An hour later I received a call from one of them. When I told him that he and another friend had entered my mind earlier that morning, he confessed that he'd contacted the other friend an hour before to get my phone number.

Perfect Timing

Another remarkable sign that speaks volumes is seeing your birth month and date on a digital clock. This often occurs during crises, especially in relationships. I have often encountered my birth date, 7:14, on clocks. I didn't understand its message clearly until I honored my intuition This sign confirmed that I needed to obey my feelings and to trust myself. It also meant that I was on the right path.

Speeding Ticket

During a volatile period in my life, as I was healing from a painful breakup, I found myself struggling to remain composed for a stretch of time. Anger dominated my days, and my actions were unconsciously abrupt and impatient.

One day after exercising at the gym, I was driving home feeling empowered, bigger than life, and unaware that I was speeding. I was pulled over and ticketed by the local police. As I sat in my car waiting for the written citation, I felt suddenly humble. I knew this event was a divine sign to slow down, be more conscious, and heal my life.

Lady Butterfly

My friend Dave received a generous inheritance from his deceased maternal grandmother. Already in the process of changing careers from the financial industry, Dave's sudden windfall provided the capital to start a landscaping business. He purchased the necessary machinery and appropriate storage and set about obtaining local clients.

While performing his duties, he noticed a white butterfly in multiple locations. After numerous butterfly experiences, he finally came to understand that his deceased grandmother was using the butterfly as a sign that she was okay, and to congratulate him on pursuing his business.

Going Home

Melanie's grandmother suddenly passed away one evening. The day after she didn't return repeated phone calls, she was discovered lying on her bed wearing the outfit she wanted to be buried in, with her dentures in her mouth. She had known she would transcend and had silently prepared herself. Her peaceful departure comforted her family.

Happy Reflection

My friend Allanah and her sister flew to Houma, Louisiana, to spend his last few days with their father who was clinging to life while suffering from lung cancer. They held his hand and shared sweet memories together until it was time to leave the hospital and head back home to Florida.

He passed away the next day. That same evening, when Allanah turned on her bathroom light, she looked in the mirror and saw her father standing behind her beaming a huge smile. Chills of happiness ran through her body. She now knows that he will always be with her and feels she has another angel watching over her.

On Track

Claire was a fun-loving, high-spirited soul who loved sports and social gatherings. During a painful breakup, she desperately needed spiritual solace. One day while driving home from work, feeling utter despair and questioning her spiritual beliefs, she yelled out, "God, where are you? I need a sign!" A split second later, as she neared a train track, the railroad-crossing light flashed once and stopped. She knew that was a divine sign that God was with her and that everything would be okay.

Greetings from Disney

Evelyn worked as a reservationist for Disney's Florida office. She had recently awakened to spiritual signs from the universe, which allowed her to live with more faith and courage. One Tuesday afternoon, while she booked reservations for a family of three, she noticed that their names sounded familiar.

Initially unsure about the familiarity, she continued arranging their plans. Then it suddenly hit her. The names were the same as those of three deceased relatives she had dreamt about the night before. She realized it was her family in the spirit world finding a creative way to say hello.

Happy Birthday

One Tuesday morning, my coworker Lara came to visit me at my desk. She was excited to tell me the story of something that had just touched her heart.

She said, "My phone rang in the middle of the night. I opened my eyes and the clock read 3:28 a.m. I lay still until the answering machine picked up, but the person didn't leave a message, so I figured it was a wrong number and fell back asleep until my alarm clock rang. When I got out of bed, I remembered that my phone had rung early that morning, so I walked into the kitchen to check the caller ID box, and unbelievably, it read, 'special message.'"

Her eyes widened as she continued, "Today is my daughter's ninth birthday. She was born at 3:28 a.m. My father was the only person in the delivery room with me, and he died less than a year ago. He loved his granddaughter so much—they had a special bond. I know he was the one who called to wish her a happy birthday."

Suggestions

- Any repeated sign is a message.
- Most messages come within your frame of reference.
- Ask for signs silently or out loud, anytime or anywhere.
- Be aware of your surroundings each day
- Déjà vu is a good sign.

CHAPTER TWENTY

SILENCE

I attended a baseball game at the legendary Yankee Stadium in the mid nineties. Hall of Famer Mickey Mantle had just passed away, and the late announcer Bob Shepherd asked that everyone stand for a moment of silence before the national anthem to pay respects to "good old Mick." I stood silently looking around the sold-out stadium of fifty thousand people and felt chills. I was astonished to see so many people standing in silence to honor a soul's legacy on earth. I could have heard a pin drop. That peaceful minute was a moment of magic to me. That feeling of awe was divine. I realized that stillness was a natural state for a soul to be in. I thought of how powerful it would be if we took time each day to honor our souls with a moment of silence.

Meditation allows your spirit to fully connect with the moment you're experiencing right now. You have plenty of time to connect with yourself. We can meditate while sitting in an airport terminal, while stuck in traffic—or how about right now? Stop reading this book, close your eyes, and just be still. Take a minute to become aware of your body, your existence, your breath. Now open your eyes and congratulate yourself—your soul was listening and thanks you for honoring it. You know how wonderful you feel when you take time to do something nice for other people? Acknowledging your own existence makes you feel just as good.

You do not have to develop any particular method of meditation. Relaxing is a form of meditation. I love to gaze at a tree, bird, or baby. I love admiring the ocean, a scenic view from a mountaintop, or the view from an airplane. I was in a semitrance when I viewed the Grand Canyon in Arizona.

I learned that deeper meditation reaped wonderful rewards as well. When my life was chaotic, I focused on deep breathing for fifteen minutes a day to release stress. It really works! My consciousness elevated, and my thoughts were less fearful and stressful. When our minds are on overdrive, ideas and thoughts can drain our energy, but we can reclaim that energy when we become aware of our breath, or our soul's presence.

When I struggle to quiet my mind, I use aromatherapy, which makes me more relaxed and focused. I usually burn sage, which helps me feel peaceful. I then feel a tingly sensation at the top of my head and know that my crown chakra is open.

Meditation is a form of prayer for me, although I may not request or focus on manifesting anything. It is a time of silence and a place of connection to my natural state of being.

Since creativity is endless, do whatever feels good for you and that helps you feel inner peace. Using astrology, meditate in the environment of your zodiac sign, your sun sign.

Fire signs (Aries, Leo, and Sagittarius): Meditate facing the sunrise or sunset, near a fireplace or a bonfire. Fire signs are a stimulated bunch and do best with short mediations.

Earth signs (Taurus, Virgo, and Capricorn): Meditate in a park, garden, or green indoor sanctuary. Also do it barefoot to stabilize and connect with Mother Earth.

Air signs (Gemini, Libra, and Aquarius): Pray or meditate in a group or with a partner. Focus on the breath, as mental focus balances out the air signs' tendency toward social and other external stimulation.

Water signs (Cancer, Scorpio, and Pisces): Meditate while soaking in a tub, sunning at the beach, or near any body of water. Drink plenty of water before and after.

Prayer

Prayer can be made in any form of communication because God— the soul of existence—is present in everything, everyone, and everywhere. Many of us were taught to say prayers aloud; however, silent prayer is just as powerful. Prayer is a form of saying, "I am divine; I am love." Anytime you acknowledge your existence or the existence of creation, you are automatically communing with God, the universe.

Prayer builds character, strengthens your spirituality, and helps you succeed in the material world. Many have had to take a leap of faith in their careers, homes, or relationships, and prayer gives them the strength and courage to make these changes with grace.

Many of us have seen dark times, since earth is the toughest of all learning dimensions. We have to face the dark before we can see the light. Prayer allows us to see the light at the end of the dark tunnel.

It is impossible to get through an earthly journey without asking or praying for assistance, because the tough energy in the physical world disrupts our path. In our temporary schoolroom on earth, every now and then we stop paying attention and get lost in the illusion of the physical world. When we are lost—when we fail to understand the teachings—all we need to do is pray and realign.

Prayer gives us permission to live in courage. Whether you're about to get behind a steering wheel or confront a challenging obstacle, request divine support or say a prayer.

Prayer, the soul's cell phone, allows you to call your spiritual family from anywhere in the physical world without ever having to charge your batteries or pay the bill. Because you carry a direct link to God, the spark of your existence, you can pray whenever, wherever, and for whatever reason.

Start a prayer journal, and list the answers or miracles that you have experienced thus far. List occasions when you have prayed for an answer, and document the outcome. When you look back, you will be astounded by the power of prayer.

Nothing is ever lost in spirit. If you prayed for a sick loved one to heal and that person died, trust that it was their destiny and that your prayers did not fall on deaf ears. All those prayers will bounce back to you in the form of support, inspiration, and other healing and loving expressions. You can never lose when it comes to prayer.

Pray for world peace, world health, and for much needed kindness. Prayer can heal anything. All prayers are heard and will serve the world and you.

The outcome of prayer, regardless of your desire, is not your concern. You do your part and then allow divine forces to do their part. When you pray passionately and detach from the outcome, your prayer is instantly transmuted. Practicing with full detachment is an act of faith, of unconditional love.

On occasion, challenging circumstances creep up and create chaos. This happens when a lesson has surfaced for us to learn. Prayer helps to quiet the distractions and keep us mentally aware. During this heightened state of listening, we are attuned to the solutions and answers we need. Never underestimate the power of prayer.

Connection

One evening while reading a book, I received a desperate phone call from a suicidal friend. Kevin had been HIV positive for a few years and was having trouble living with the diagnosis. He was mentally exhausted and wanted to give up and end his life. As gently as I could, I told him that these thoughts would pass and advised him not to act on them. He abruptly ended our conversation, saying he no longer had the energy to talk.

Deep in my soul, I knew he would not end his life. However, his depressed state alarmed me deeply, so I lit a candle, closed my eyes, and prayed for his life. I specifically asked, "God, please lift Kevin's depression and restore his peace of mind." I said this request three times out loud.

There was something special about this prayer. When I opened my eyes, I felt light-headed, as if I had tapped into a higher divine vibration. There was power in the minute of *silence* that followed. A trusting peace came over me. The clock showed 8:00 p.m. I decided to wait an hour before calling Kevin to check up on him. I returned to my book.

Forty-five minutes later Kevin called back. His voice was full of peace, illumination, and gratitude, and he apologized for alarming me. I immediately started to cry. I was overwhelmed by his new humility and the miracle of my prayer. Kevin told me he'd felt extremely drained from the psychological turmoil and had decided to lie down and rest. He'd felt a peaceful feeling come over him that had eliminated his destructive thoughts. He said, "I was literally *touched* by an angel." I told him I had lit a candle and sent out a powerful prayer, which must have been answered instantaneously

The Burning Message

My sister, Alexis, invited me to her house for a winter solstice ceremony. Her friend Darlene, a psychic who comes from a long line of Wiccans, facilitated a pagan ritual, as she does every year.

The participants sat on pillows on the living room floor around a roaring fireplace. The ritual began with a candle ceremony and a prayer to the universe. We each held a twelve-inch taper in a glass holder. We added spiritual herbs and oils to our candles so that when we lit them, their spiritual vibrations would be released into the universe.

We then held the intent of love in our hearts and wrote down our hopes, wishes, and desires on bay leaves. We repeated each message twice on separate leaves. We added one set to our candle, completing our creative decorations. We burned the other set, sending our intensions into the universe to create that manifestation. Nobody in the group knew any other's written intentions—we kept them to ourselves.

We each took turns burning our bay leaves in an ashtray. When my turn came, I grabbed the tip of the leaf closest to the stem and lit the other end with a lighter. I watched the flame trickle along the length of each leaf. The speed at which it burned seemed to indicate how quickly that intention would become manifest. One leaf in particular flamed up immediately and dissolved into ash within three seconds. Everyone gasped in wonder, including Darlene. On that leaf I'd written, "Grow closer to God."

However, my last leaf did not want to burn. The flame kept going out. I had to relight it ten times before it burned out completely. That wish was "to be in a romantic relationship." It was a strong sign that I needed to focus on my inner spark of God and put romance on the back burner for awhile.

After our leaf-burning ritual, Darlene passed around a bag of votive candles in multiple colors, each wrapped with an inscribed prayer. The votive candle I chose was green. The message read, "Please allow the innate healing energies, which divinity provide for everyone, to surface and heal myself and others."

We concluded with a half-hour meditation. Alexis played soothing music, and we all sprawled comfortably across the floor and visualized our intentions. The experience was beautiful and magical, and I hardly noticed that two hours had gone by.

Suggestions

- Meditation helps connect to your true self.
- Prayer always helps anything.
- Silence is a peaceful state of being.

- Sleep helps restore and renew the body, mind, and emotions.
- Spiritual rituals keep you centered.
- Your feelings are to be trusted—your heart is not only the beat of your physical life but it is also the divine cord to your spiritual life.

CHAPTER TWENTY-ONE

THOUGHTS

The mind is a divine instrument that is fittingly positioned at the highest point of the physical body, closest to the sky. A transparent funnel sits atop the head—this is also called the *crown chakra*—through which creative thoughts and inspiration can penetrate from above. To receive impressions, ideas, wisdom, creative and constructive thoughts, we need to make sure we don't clog up the funnel. We keep it clear by minimizing drama, judgment, and anger. It is up to us to maintain a clean filter, or an open mind, and we can do this with mental awareness.

While it is important to verbally express your thoughts and feelings, it is just as important to quiet the mind and pay attention. One of my favorite quotes comes from a cartoon called "Meet Mr. Luckey" by Henri Arnold, printed in the sports section of the New York *Daily News*. It says, "A closed mouth is often evidence of an open mind."

One of the most important relationships you'll experience during your earthly journey is the one with your thoughts and feelings.

When you are aware of both your thoughts and feelings, you are awake and empowered. The choice to feel good, peaceful, or happy starts with your thoughts. Although our minds flutter like a butterfly from time to time, an awareness of what we are thinking is the catalyst for our feelings.

Thought such as sadness, anger, and betrayal drain the emotions. This low vibrational mind-set is the ego's playground—victimization! On many days I drove home from work feeling drained. I'd repeatedly replay negative scenarios of office drama, boyfriend issues, lack of financial abundance, or whatever empowered the ego.

On these days, I'd pull into my parking spot and not remember the drive home. I was so consumed with negative thoughts—what a waste of time. There's no need to fight these thoughts; all you can do is acknowledge that your ego is engaged, and this awareness will stop the unconscious Broadway show. Your mind is a stage, so conscious thoughts of humor, creativity, parties, concerts, friends, food, pets, or sex will keep you entertained, positively. Music is a great distracter from ego. Try singing along to the radio while you're driving.

Positive thoughts are similar to blue skies. When the sky is sunny, its reflection is evident on any body of water. In the same way, positive thoughts reflect healthy emotions. If you're unhappy or tormented by negative thoughts, it is the illusion, fear, or judgment that you need to transform. You can only do this with conscious awareness.

Hearing our own spoken words clearly, especially when we're engaged in a meaningful discussion, is an awakened experience. These are times when we're really aware of our thoughts. While channeling and interpreting astrology charts, I'd clearly hear my voice give definitive answers and guidance to someone's life, which unexpectedly answered my own questions or settled my own conflicts at the time.

The more conscious we are, the more available we are to the universe, and the more we become instruments to others and ourselves.

Challenges and Obstacles

We have the free will to live as freely as possible, and that requires awareness of blocks and limitations that keep you from expressing your talents and gifts. The law of cause and effect is alive and well. When I was twenty, I suffered from sleep deprivation, depression, and claustrophobia. I went to see a psychologist to help me through it. During our weekly sessions, he often mentioned the classic analogy of peeling back an onion one layer at a time to get to the core of my problem. After three months of therapy, I felt a little better. I'd learned that I had fear of rejection—but this didn't *cure* my symptoms, it just dimmed them.

When I finally grew tired of focusing on my symptoms, I realized I was unconsciously creating them. Since thoughts are energy, I created what I focused upon. When I was finally true to my sexual orientation and came out of the closet, all of my symptoms vanished. If I had still focused on eliminating one symptom at a time, I would still be in therapy. I corrected the effects by eliminating the cause, or replacing a fear with a truth. The correction was all mental.

Challenges, obstacles, and lessons are triggered by one of two reasons—a lack of concentration, or a lack of education. The answer to either one is *awareness*.

Lack of concentration is self-explanatory. If we're not watching where we're walking, especially up or down steps, we can trip and hurt ourselves. If we're not paying attention while we are driving, we can cause an accident. If we're not conscious of our words and behavior, we can unconsciously hurt another.

Lack of education is the cause of most of our suffering. There are many things we don't know but will be guided to learn during the earthly incarnation. The idea that we each have an ego is important to know because the ego can be a great source of pain and suffering, so to acknowledge it gives you the power to not live in it.

As stated before, the ego loves to play the victim, and it feeds off of guilt and punishment. One of the toughest lessons to learn is self-criticism, which often happens when we don't know the reason behind something and we become angry with ourselves for not knowing. This behavior is common to those who've had tough childhoods and whose guardians didn't make them feel secure or guided. When you suffer from childhood insecurities, you feel there's no more room for error, so you unconsciously punish yourself for not knowing and cause yourself more pain. This is ego behavior, but luckily, it can be changed through awareness.

As a natural leader, I like to be in control and to have things flow smoothly. When obstacles and challenges arise, I can get frustrated and stressed out. When I chill out and surrender my destructive ego behavior, the answer reveals itself. It's not easy not to react calmly at times, but if I stay conscious and regain a state of peace, empowerment and the answers usually surface. The reaction to an obstacle is the pathway to the solution.

Regaining peace is saying to the universe, "I am a student and willing to learn." Losing your cool is definitely the reaction of the victim—the ego. It is a way of saying, "Why me?" It's important to silence the inner critic. Stress ages the body; let's not rush the aging process. I now laugh more and criticize myself less. Awareness is working.

Sometimes we disregard our intuition and go through a painful experience. It is very easy to beat ourselves up and allow the ego voice of self-criticism take over. Please do not speak negatively to yourself at all. It is important to know that even if you knew better but acted on temptation, impulse, or unhealthy habit, you can still lovingly correct your error without punish yourself.

Look into a mirror and lovingly forgive yourself for the unsavory or painful choice. This will expedite the healing. Looking into the mirror and speaking kindly to yourself is an act of self-love and doesn't give the ego space for any more negativity.

We can often learn much under duress because sudden events wake us up or elevate our consciousness. It is important to keep an open mind and seek knowledge during challenging times. How many of us agonized over a failed intimate relationship, only to view it later on has a blessing in disguise, a valuable lesson learned, or a necessary stepping-stone for our life partner? When we make the psychological change to view a hardship as a learning opportunity, we cease to resist and flow with the lesson, which also mitigates emotional pain.

It's very common to feel uncomfortable through stretches of life, and that's okay. You are not from this planet: like all of us, you are only experiencing it temporarily. It's difficult to be conscious every waking second. Whenever a challenge or obstacle surfaces, know there are lessons to learn, an invitation for growth, and that you can achieve a serenity once again.

Your soul is divine and perfect. Try to laugh at past ego behavior, especially if you've overreacted, so you can remember that everything is fine and that challenges are temporary.

Positive Affirmations

Focused positive affirmations are some of the most empowering actions you can exercise to program the mind. While reading Louise L. Hay's *You Can Heal Your Life*, I followed the guidance and practiced one of the affirmations while looking into my eyes in a mirror. I repeated the affirmation often and noticed that my voice changed during each repetition. I realized that I was trying to sell my subconscious on something that I hadn't bought yet. This awareness made me laugh heartily at myself. After a good belly laugh I finally started to believe in what I was affirming and sounded more confident. Speaking out loud helps you hear your words and brings awareness to your thoughts. Most of our limitations are mental, and positive affirmations can change them. How awesome!

Many self-help books reiterate a similar message—that mental focus or controlled thought is the key to positive mental transformation. Discipline, drive, and direction keeps the ego in check.

Positive affirmations help to eliminate negative thoughts patterns and awaken you to the truth that you are wonderful and worthy. Gracefully let go of fear-based thoughts, and replace them with positive affirmations. By transforming your thoughts, you can transform your life.

There are times we get enlighten by sudden insight and we instantaneously change an old unhealthy thought pattern. Other times, the mental reprogramming can be a process, especially a victim consciousness. It's analogous to a messy construction site because of widening roads. When we broaden our minds and expand a narrow view point, it can take time, but the larger perspective will allow the mind's traffic to flow easier.

Mental preparation, discipline, or affirmations will ensure a high probability of success. Successful athletes, especially baseball pitchers, have mental routines they use to prepare for their games. Their body language and facial expressions reflect their focus, and prepare them to perform at a high level. Authors, entertainers, and other artists have also created similar mental routines in order to increase their chances of success. You can only increase your chance of being happy if you aware, disciplined, and positive.

Thoughts (with feelings) are invisible sparks of light that send energy to their destinations. Whenever we view a photo, especially of a loved one, we send them a silent message.

Just envisioning a person or pet sends them a mental impression, so send positive and loving thoughts to others. Your mind is powerful. Be conscious, be happy, and think positively.

The Brain

The left side of the brain, which rules rationality and logic, allows us to understand science, including psychology. Spirituality and emotion are housed in the right side of the brain, which rules creativity and imagination. Both sides complement each other and keep the mind balanced.

People are captivated by stories, especially if they teach meaningful lessons. Many wonderful authors have channeled their creative juices into writing entertaining and compelling books.

Opening statements in court cases can tell compelling stories and captivate jurors' attention. It's all in how the story is told.

I believe we are becoming more creative as a society, and it shows in our architecture, our medical and technological advances, and our spiritual movements. All of these and other wonderful expansions are creations of the human brain—of visions or thoughts. It is wonderful to know that we are all receptors of endless divine impressions for creation and evolution. The potential to create is boundless.

Humor also requires creativity. For example, whenever I'm asked, "Are you married?" or" Do you have children?", I usually reply, "Yes, I'm married. I've tried having children with my male partner, but he hasn't gotten pregnant yet." After an initial shock, my listener usually gets it and laughs.

When my hair started to gray, especially at my sideburns and chin, it complemented my dark brown hair. I gracefully looked in the mirror one day and said, "Salt-and-pepper hair means I'm well-seasoned." My creative viewpoint helped me to accept nature's physical evolution.

It is estimated that our brains absorb and send out sixty thousand ideas a day. When a friend recently asked me if I had ever experienced writer's block, I said no. Ideas are infinite, and since our minds are connected to the universe, thoughts never end. If I receive no more ideas for a specific chapter or page, then I move on to the next chapter or page and introduce the next idea.

Try the following exercise to clear your mind and allow creative and innovative thoughts to enter: Lie down in the grass on a clear night. Look up and envision the sky as your mind. See it as open, clear, and endless. Next, see the stars and envision them as thoughts, with each blinking light a creative idea or vision. Then look at the empty area between the stars and imagine that vast amount of space as the infinite potential of your mind.

Daily Living

I was recently delayed on a flight from Newark Airport in New Jersey because of rainy weather. When I finally boarded the plane, I looked forward to taking off. It took only four and a half minutes for the plane to ascend above the clouds and into a beautiful blue sky with bright sunshine. As I looked out the window, I had a wonderful revelation: the sun is always shining and the sky is always blue, regardless of the day's *appearance*. What I initially *perceived* to be a lousy day turned out to be a beautiful day in *reality*.

This analogy can be applied to our minds and thoughts. Whenever our thoughts turn gloomy, we need to remember that the sun is always shining brightly, and on occasion, we need to rise above the clouds and move our thoughts toward a spiritual perspective in order to see the light, the truth. I now view rainy days as reminders to clean out my thought filter and allow the sun to shine through. If it took a large metal plane only four and a half minutes to rise above the rain, think about how fast we can change our thoughts.

Patience is a mental discipline. Everyone has experienced travel delays due to traffic, accidents, or inclement weather. Eventually, the obstacle will clear; however, the experience can be frustrating or peaceful depending on our mind-set. View delays as part of the life plan, especially when you have no control over the action. When I heard stories of delays, especially from survivors from 9/11, I realized that delays can be a blessing. Accept what you can't control. Mental patience is a learned discipline. Ask any woman who is pregnant and overdue.

Listening is an attribute of mental discipline. We can learn something every day by listening. The universe always provides mental impressions and inspiration, and your awareness determines how you assimilate and express these thoughts.

Everything starts with a mental impression and ends with a mental expression, so constructive verbal communication is important in our daily lives. When our thoughts are in harmony with our emotions, we articulate clearly and share meaningful conversation. We need to respect our verbal abilities and not abuse, overuse, or disrespect them. The words we speak matter.

I enjoy speaking to seniors about what they have learned in their lives. A few years back, I had a meaningful conversation with an 83-year-old lady, a recent widow, who had driven 1,400 miles from Michigan to Florida to visit friends. While sipping her martini, she smiled and said, "Your life is dictated by how you feel, and how you feel depends on how you think." Truer words were never spoken.

The Life Script

Everyone has divine triggers in their charts. Fated events will occur. They are designed to awaken our thoughts and help us expand. Sometimes they catch us off guard, and we initially react with fear. It's okay to feel upset, but it's not favorable to remain upset for a long period of time. During these times, we need to regain our composure and see everything through spiritual eyesight. We must think in a spiritual terms to avoid being victimized by adverse circumstances.

There is a purpose, there is a mission, and everything will be revealed in divine time. All you need to do is be open-minded and think spiritually. One of my favorite quotes from *A Course in Miracles* is, "The power of one mind can shine into another, because all the lamps of God were lit by the same spark. It is everywhere and it is eternal."

Don't just survive—live! Love; you can't lose! Laugh; the tears come anyway! Liberate; you don't have to carry the load alone! Listen; the answers will reveal themselves in divine time! Learn; the lessons are worth it!

Suggestions

- Think before speaking. Actors and actresses have to read their scripts before they play their parts. In our solar system, Mercury, the planet of communication, comes before Mars, the planet of action.
- To renew and replenish your mind, head to the beach, park, or mountains regularly.
- You succeed when you focus your mind, so choose to be happy, lucky, blessed, grateful, and loved.
- Opening your mind is like opening your window blinds or curtains to let the sunshine in. Sunlight through an open mind brings many sunny thoughts.
- Keep a journal of happy memories. When you reminisce, your mind will be filled with love and joy.
- Remember the three C's: conscious, creative, and constructive.
- You can create a great life. You have the power, and it all begins with a thought.

CHAPTER TWENTY-TWO

PURPOSE

Your soul's purpose is to learn lessons on earth, and your spiritual mission is to express your talents and gifts. In simpler terms, your purpose is to receive, and your mission is to give.

When we know that our purpose is to receive and our mission is to give, then our life *feels* meaningful. When you are learning and growing, you feel better about yourself, and when you can help or teach, the feeling is priceless.

Earth is not just a classroom for academic lessons. You are here to learn about emotions and sensations too. You are here to live a conscious life so you can see, feel, and believe firsthand the power of spirit within the physical world. The greatest feeling we can experience is the awareness of our essence, our true divine selves.

Dharma, Sanskrit for "law of the universe," is a concept in Hinduism and Buddhism. It also means "life's purpose." *Karma*, another Sanskrit term, means "law of cause and effect" and "action, work, or deeds." When you are learning lessons (purpose) and expressing your knowledge, talents, or gifts (mission), you are living according to the law of the universe (dharma) and will reap the rewards (karma).

If you are led to a mentor, it is highly probable that you were spiritually guided to develop or to awaken specific talents or truths that will aid you in your spiritual mission. Whether it's a book or a personal seminar, honor that mentor's attributes, and remember you are a creative and unique expression of God, so incorporate your personality, your essence, into your lessons, and be your own mentor too. Then you can teach others and give them permission to be creative in their own mentorship. In the evolution of life, the apprentice exceeds the mentor, and the cycle expands. Olympic records are often broken by new and improved athletes. We are meant to exceed, expand, and evolve. We do not need to pattern our lives after anyone. We are like the stars in the sky: we already have our light, and it naturally shines bright.

During a meaningful phone conversation about life with a close friend one evening, a profound statement he made regarding life enlightened me: "You can't keep track of your life journey through years, only through experiences." If one looks closely, it is one's experiences that characterize one's journey, and those experiences are part of your soul's purpose.

Knowledge is infinite and so are the lessons. We all have a purpose and a mission. Your existence is priceless. View yourself as a divine instrument in the heavenly orchestra. Without your harmony, the band wouldn't sound as good. You matter, and the universe does support you.

Nobel Peace Prize winner Albert Schweitzer said, "We make a living by what we get, but we make a life by what we give."

Nature Beings

I received many revelations about life one afternoon while sitting outside on my deck. The element of air and its purpose interested me. Air is made up of gases—unseen by the human eye but felt by the human body. I noticed how my body reacted when a breeze swept over me: my awareness heightened, and I felt gratitude for the boost of oxygen—a sustainer of life. I also found it interesting how stagnant and lifeless I felt when there was no breeze—it was as though someone had turned off the flow of energy. Notice how welcome a refreshing breeze feels on a hot and humid summer's day. The flow of air can either elevate or lower your mood. Life is better and happier when we feel the flow of the energy of life.

I then witnessed how the air affected the plants, especially rustling the leaves of a big old oak tree. I could outline the different sources of the air as it flowed through the branches by the fact that some leaves remained still while other leaves moved with ease in the direction that the breeze dictated. This same life force that flowed through the tree is the force that flows through us. We flow with the varying energy because we are vibrating at different frequencies. We, and all beings in nature, are connected.

I next focused on the tree's trunk and received another truth. Every tree is rooted in earth, but each grows at a different speed to a different size and color. We are all children of God, rooted in the spirit of love, but we're all physically different, and these differences make us beautiful. An oak tree is different from a palm tree, but they both radiate a beautiful uniqueness.

One day while meditating in my home, I opened my eyes and was guided to stare at the philodendron plant in front of me. Within seconds I witnessed a miracle: a new leaf sprang forth, one quick motion, and it was still curled up. The *birth* shook the entire stem from which it emanated while the rest of the plant remained still. This event still amazes me.

Roses vary in color and are symbols of love. Their thorns remind us that something as precious as they are is divinely protected and needs to be handled gently. We are just as delicate and beautiful as roses.

Birds are fun to watch, and they too have a purpose. There are different species in many sizes and colors. They exemplify love because love is free, and they fly so freely. Also, if they're to fly, they can't have any weight—baggage—attached to their wings. Can you imagine a bird trying to fly with small suitcases hanging from its wings? We need to follow suit by eliminating fear, prejudice, judgment, drama, and worries in order to freely fly and live in true love.

Song is the fulfillment of a bird's life purpose, and humans too each have a song to sing. Singing is a bird's innate desire, and it keeps their souls joyful and enlivens with sweet music. I watched a bird build a nest one twig one time. I was amazed by all that work; it reminded me of this journey on earth. We each have a part to play, a mission to accomplish, on this planet—your existence is not a random act. Every one of us has a divine script, a meaningful plan.

The purpose of nature's variety is to teach us how to live.

Cosmic Beings

In astrology, the sun represents the father, and is therefore masculine, and the intellect, and the moon represents the mother, and is therefore feminine, and emotion. The sun's awesome light illuminates everything; it warms the planet and makes things grow. The moon is quite powerful in the dark, where she works behind the scenes, illuminating the dark skies and regulating the tides.

Look up to the sky and see the space between all the blinking lights. They reflect you. Everyone is given the space they need to shine brightly! Notice that the lights blink at their own frequencies, some brighter than others. Yet they are all part of, not separate from, the same universe. Cosmic beings have an abundance of light, space, and love—and this holds true for human beings. They all serve a purpose (you do not have to be an astrologer or astronomer to know this), and so do we. There is more abundance than you can conceive of. There is no lack. The birth of these celestial bodies was not a random act, and neither is your life.

Life, like the solar system, is ruled by cycles. The planets orbit the sun and complete a cycle, only to repeat it. We must awaken to the reality that we are given opportunity after opportunity to learn and grow. If we do not awaken, the specific lessons will repeat themselves because everything happens in cycles. Open to your divine existence—receive, give, and live a wonderful life.

Human Beings

A plaque that hangs in my home office bears twenty-one suggestions for success written by H. Jackson Brown Jr. My favorite is, "Understand that happiness is not based on possessions, power or prestige, but on relationships with people you love and respect."

Part of your purpose is to engage in relationships with others because the exchange of energy—love—is what keeps you aligned, connected, and happy. It doesn't cost anything to relate to another, and you have everything to gain when you do. The source of my true happiness is my relationships, especially my friendships. The exchange of energy with friends is priceless. No amount of money can bring you that connection and joy. This is an important truth to living a great life on earth. When you love your life and the people in it, you feel like you don't need anything. Now that's happiness!

As we learn spiritual lessons on earth, we have human experiences through our bodies. Another truth for living an improved, happier, and more fantastic life is physical pleasure. The body feels great after a good laugh, a workout, a shower, a meal, sleep, or sex. All these pleasures makes the body *feel* good and makes the arduous earthly journey bearable. You are not your body, but you were given this temporary structure to fulfill your purpose, and feelings are important! So make your body feel rested, nourished, and gratified. Don't fear it—embrace it, talk to it, touch it, and love it. Provide for its needs, and it will serve you well.

Releasing limitations allows you to receive. When you can accept that part of your purpose is to experience abundance, you will laugh and laugh and enjoy your life beyond illusionary limitations. Whatever you fear or hurt, I urge you to heal by identifying the cause and taking action to correct it. Remember that emotional pain is only a teaching tool that is to be felt and then released.

Believe in people, places, and things that bring about harmony, love, and unity since we are all created with the same energy. Ever notice how conscious you become when a life-changing event, sudden tragedy, or trauma gets your attention? We all truly see, feel, and believe the power of spirit under duress regardless of what our physical bodies look like. When help comes, accept it. We are all one.

When we live a consciously awakened life, we are more likely to treat others in well. Awareness is an understanding that we all feel pain and we all are learning lessons, and treating others and ourselves with kindness and compassion is the way of love. Feeling superior or mistreating others is ego behavior and can lead to painful experiences because we are one and the same, and the law of cause and effect or karma is alive and well. I've experienced this myself and I've seen it come back to others.

Our respect for each other increases when we don't allowing our differences to dim our true lights. We steadily progress with more awareness. This is evident in ever-increasing laws against discrimination. The most exciting time one can experience is the present because it's the only time that's real. Smile awareness is right now. That's empowerment!

Human suffering or despair is a lack of awareness. We regain our happiness when we learn. If earth is our schoolroom, then we must be here to educate. The willingness to do so will align you with your purpose.

It is never too late to awaken to your dreams and to honor your feelings, your heart's desires. Live an abundant, loving life filled with opportunities. Talents and desires don't go away with time. In fact, they grow stronger because they need to be *expressed*, not repressed. You gain more energy when you fulfill your creative talents and your heart's desires. They are gifts to humanity.

The schoolroom of earth is abundant. We have many tools and resources at our disposal. To think that God created one ascended master for the whole planet is humorous. If that were the case, then God would have created one piece of land, one body of water, one planet, one star. There are many wonderful spiritual teachers who have walked the earth and fulfilled their spiritual missions by teaching, awakening, and reminding us that we have the power. We are created from the same fabric. We possess the answers. Trust your heart, and you will find that we are all *truly* one.

Misconceptions and misperceptions leave us uneasy, like square pegs trying to fit into round holes. Question ambiguity, and filter everything you read or hear through your head and heart to arrive at the truth. Your intuition is alive and well and is always available. When something rings true, it resonates. Go with that feeling! It is the answer or will lead you to the answer.

Plants, trees, birds, humans, planets, stars, books, and cars exist in all shapes, colors, and sizes. Zoos wouldn't exist if not for the myriad animals on earth. Clouds serve many purposes: they produce rain, shade on a hot summer's day, and reflect the light of a beautiful sunset. They too come in many shapes, sizes, and shades. The produce area in a grocery store displays many fruits and vegetables of many sizes and colors. Trust that everyone has a purpose, and a mission, and that we are all one.

Suggestions

- Earth is a schoolroom, and your life is an incarnation to learn lessons of the heart for your soul's evolution. Earth is one of the most challenging dimensions in creation, but it's also the most gratifying place to learn, grow, and evolve the most.
- Peace of mind comes from knowing the truth.
- Don't live life with a sense of urgency, live with a sense of purpose.
- Keep learning and expanding your mind.
- Astrology and numerology are great scientific tools to identify your spiritual purpose and mission.

- Treat yourself with respect, compassion, and forgiveness. Believe that you are part of, not separate from, the universe.
- View yourself as a student, not a victim, and learn gracefully.
- Have reverence for seniors. Wrinkles and spots on the skin of people, like fruit, show us that they are mature and ripe.
- Laugh as often as you can.
- Character-building experiences (challenges) are the roots from which your oak tree grows, the foundation upon which your house is built, and the legs upon which your tables and chairs stand. They awaken, strengthen, and sustain your spiritual existence so you can withstand the illusion of the physical.
- Look at life as being in college. We need to take some courses as prerequisites that are not appealing to us. Don't rebel against them; instead view them as requirements for graduation, for fulfilling your soul's purpose on earth.
- Soul mates come in many forms: parents, siblings, friends, lovers, children, and pets.
- Healing from a challenging childhood is your avenue to your joy.
- When you know better, you will do better.
- A Smile is the sign of an open heart, and open hearts attract other open hearts. The law of attraction guarantees it.
- Pray for signs and guidance toward your purpose and mission.
- Express your emotions and honor your feelings—they are a gateway to a fulfilled life.
- Read *The Life You Were Born to Live* by Dan Millman.
- Live a conscious life, and marvel at your existence. Your spirit is awesome.
- Experience life, don't escape it.
- Do what you're good at. It builds confidence and self-esteem.
- Try to forgive everyone.
- Seek academic training in a subject you love.
- Listen to your dreams.
- Be creative.

- Spend quiet time alone. Creative silence is wonderful.
- Change is a natural part of life, like leaves falling from trees, hair falling from our heads, and the dead skin cells falling from our bodies.
- Your heart knows love, desire, peace, joy, wisdom, and purpose.

Bibliography

Colgrove, Melba, Ph.D., Harold H. Bloomfield, M.D. and Peter McWilliams. *How to Survive the Loss of a Love*. Los Angeles: Prelude Press, 1991.

Foundation for Inner Peace. *A Course in Miracles*. Mill Valley, CA, 1996.

Hay, Louise L. *You Can Heal Your Life*. Carlsbad, CA: Hay House, 1999.

Hicks, Esther, and Jerry Hicks. *The Law of Attraction*. Carlsbad, CA: Hay House, 2006.

MacLaine, Shirley. *Out on a Limb*. New York: Bantam Books, 1983.

Millman, Dan. *The Life You Were Born to Live*. San Rafael, CA: New World Library, 1993.

Peale, Norman Vincent. *The Power of Positive Thinking*. New York: Fawcett Crest, 1956.

Van Praagh, James. *Talking to Heaven.* New York: Dutton, 1997.

Virtue, Doreen. *Archangels and Ascended Masters.* Carlsbad, CA: Hay House, 2003.

Virtue, Doreen. *The Lightworker's Way.* Carlsbad, CA: Hay House, 1997.

Virtue, Doreen, and Lynnette Brown. *Angel Numbers.* Carlsbad, CA: Hay House, 2005.

Weiss, Brian L. *Many Lives, Many Masters.* New York: Fireside Books, 1988.

Williamson, Marianne. *A Return to Love.* New York: HarperCollins, 1992.